AT THE FOOT OF THE TREE

by the same author

**ON THE SHRED
OF A
CLOUD**

(The University of Alabama Press, 1969)

AT THE FOOT OF THE TREE

a wanderer's musings
before the fall

by
Rolf Edberg

translated by
David Mel Paul and Margareta Paul

THE UNIVERSITY OF ALABAMA PRESS
University, Alabama

The translators acknowledge their indebtedness to the following published works: the King James Version of the Bible (epigraph to chapter 1); *The Collected Poems of Kathleen Raine*, London, 1956 (epigraph to chapter 2); "The Apocrypha" in *The New English Bible*, New York, 1970 (epigraph to chapter 4); *Albert Einstein: A Documentary Biography*, by Carl Seelig, tr. by Mervin Savill, London, 1956 (quotations in chapter 5 and epigraph to chapter 6); *Goethe's Satyrus and Prometheus*, transl. by John Gray, Glasgow, 1898 (epigraph to chapter 8); and *The Elder Edda: A Selection*, tr. by Paul B. Taylor and W. H. Auden, New York, 1970 (the sibylline prophecy quoted in chapter 8 from verse 41 of "Song of the Sibyl").

Translated into English from **Vid Trädets Fot**
Copyright © 1971 by Rolf Edberg
Published by P. A. Norstedt & Söners Förlag
Stockholm, Sweden

English translation and addenda copyright © 1974
by The University of Alabama Press

ISBN 0-8173-6614-8
Library of Congress Catalog Card Number 73-7454

All rights reserved
Manufactured in the United States of America

Contents

Translators' Preface

AUTUMN WANDERING

1 "Wander over the autumnal earth . . ." 3
2 "The path inward—a path back . . ." 9
3 "In the beginning, the word was not . . ." 34

LOOKING, WITH CALM IN OUR HEARTS, AT ALL THAT SURROUNDS US

4 "You, there! . . . Who are you? . . ." 51
5 "It is only you that dies . . ." 75

SOLIDARITY WITH LIFE

6 "Our species became *Homo technicus* . . ." 99
7 "The brain is like a wood . . ." 124
8 "The world-tree sways . . ." 140

Bibliographical Note

To Astrid

*To return to the root is
to find peace.*
>> The Book of Tao

TRANSLATORS' PREFACE

- Staring rapt into the electron microscope, I watched a scientist step deeper and deeper into the weird world of the virus, half creature and half molecule. Was it really possible to say just where he crossed the border between life and nonlife?
- Astonished and troubled, I looked at a frog that was looking back at me—with three eyes. A researcher had transplanted an eye into the top of its head while it was still in embryo. Where was the limit to man's ability to manipulate living flesh?
- Talking with the man who had just broken the genetic code, I wondered: if it was only the sequence of code units that fated me to be a man instead of a mantis, weren't both us predators pretty close cousins? Having deciphered the code, wouldn't men soon be trying to send their own—maybe predatory—messages? . . .

. . . In 1961, few had seen these things, and for half a decade to come hardly anyone would be asking these questions out loud.

In Sweden, Rolf Edberg broke that silence. His 1966 book *Spillran av ett moln,* published in English under the title *On the Shred of a Cloud* (University of Alabama Press, 1969), showed that misapplication of biology's new powers would be the logical next step for a species that had already pillaged earth's resources, poisoned ocean, land, and sky, and traded the balance of nature for military technology's balance of terror.

It was this book, primarily, that stirred the Swedes to press for what eventually became the United Nations World Conference on the Human Environment, convened in Stockholm in June, 1972—not because Edberg said what no one else had ever thought, but because he said straight out what many had only begun to sense, and saw connections that most had only begun to glimpse. Political tyranny, poverty, overpopulation, environmental degradation, war and the threat of atomic annihilation, Edberg pointed out, are all facets of a single adamantine problem. It is our fragmented view of things that causes us to respond to the problem so diffusely and so ineffectually. If only we could achieve a unified and unifying view of man and his role in the universe, Edberg suggested, it might lead us to new human institutions on the same world scale as the threats to man, and enable us to cope with the central problem of man's nature.

But what *is* man's true nature, and what *is* his real role in the universe? In 1971, Edberg confronted these questions with *Vid trädets fot,* the book on which this revised and updated translation is based.

These questions must have a special urgency for a man whose years (Edberg is sixty-one) constrain him to begin facing the certainty of his own dissolution, and whose experience convinces him that mankind, too, confronts the possibility of its dissolution—if it does not act fast to avert disaster. His search for answers leads him back through time, before history, to life's incredible and yet fated first appearance on earth. He finds valuable clues in the experiences of tree-climbing primates, and in the social cohesion of primitive man's hunting packs.

He considers language, the double-edged weapon that became the tool that shaped man even as man was shaping it—language, which in transmitting man's civilization has given us a "new set of genes." Edberg ranges freely from death's social history to the symptoms of consciousness in insignificant amoeba and inconceivable nebula. He scouts the frontiers of biochemistry and cell biology, paleontology and ethology, historical linguistics, anthropology, and depth psychology. Out of the perspectives on mankind's experience that these sciences provide, out of his own life experience, and out of the grim prognoses of the future that current events suggest, he builds a compelling argument for an explicit crisis program to avert mankind's imminent catastrophe. It is a measure of the man as of the book that, en route, he discovers reason for joy, and not despair, at the inevitable dissolution of each individual life, and reason for hope as to mankind's prospects.

The man began his journey in 1912, in the Swedish province of Värmland. The profession he chose was journalism, but the Social Democratic party was building its present power and needed his talent. He served in the Swedish parliament in 1941–44 and 1949–56. It was during the later term that he made his first trip to the United States, a tour of seventeen states to study the various forms of American municipal administration. He also continued in journalism, becoming the editor of *Ny Tid*, a daily newspaper, and president of the Swedish Press Club. Meanwhile, he represented Sweden in the Nordic Council, the Council of Europe, and the United Nations, and, from 1961 to 1965, was alternate chairman of the Swedish delegation to the Disarmament Conference. He was appointed Sweden's ambassador to Norway, serving there eleven years. Since 1967 he has been the governor of his native province.

Meeting Rolf Edberg, one guesses at a proud nature that has had to bend itself to patience and humility. Working with him, one visualizes his mind as a Gothic arch, in which an infinitude of details are subordinated to the imperative reaching upward and upward toward some higher vantage point from which to survey experience, existence. If occasionally a detail refuses to be subordinated, if he sometimes seems to be straining rather than reaching, nevertheless the bravery and sublimity of his overarching intention deserve our respect and frequently compel our admiration.

Margareta and I have felt privileged indeed to translate Rolf Edberg's new book into English. A work that ranges so widely draws on a variety of special technical vocabularies, and an author so richly educated draws his allusions from many literatures. Hence we have sought, and are grateful for, the advice of friends, scientists, and scholars. Among these are Professor Doctor Bruno F. Steinbruckner of the American Goethe Society, Doctors Richard Hewlett and George L. Rogosa of the United States Atomic Energy Commission, Mr. Eric A. Vadelund of the United States Bureau of Standards, Doctor Raymond L. Nace of the Geological Survey of the United States Department of the Interior, Doctor Kwang Tsing Wu of the Chinese and Korean Section at the Library of Congress, and Mr. James O'Neill and Mrs. Gunilla Da Ponte of the District of Columbia Public Library. Finally, we would like to thank Mr. Sven Åhman for allowing us to quote from his unpublished translation of Lucretius' *On the Nature of Things.*

Washington, D.C. DAVID MEL PAUL
May, 1973

AUTUMN WANDERING

I

> *My root was spread out by the waters,*
> *and the dew lay all night on my branch.*
> Book of Job

WANDER OVER THE AUTUMNAL EARTH. Go there and unleaf your mind.

The air is acid. The daylight has a sharpness that brings everything near. The sun hangs low, its light enfeebled. Gaunt branches draw their stark black strokes against a pale sky.

To wander over the autumnal earth is to encounter chill, stillness, and the earth's heavy odors. How the encounter turns out depends on what you are looking for, or whether you are looking for something. Autumn has its own compass. It points to summing up and insight. If you follow that course, meeting the stillness and the odors of decay becomes a meeting that has the weight of something inescapable, natural, and near.

Just now, on the same ground, in the autumn's first phase of hectic blazing, in the busy time of preparations and leave takings:

The foliage burned in sulfur and rust, umber and blood, with lingering traces of tired green. The color patches were capriciously daubed on rough backdrops, ridge beyond ridge of green-black pine wood. Mushrooms puffed up out of the ground, sought the day in violent but slack ardor, doughy swelling of earth's bitter juices. Plants heavy with seed sank down toward the earth to will their last fruits into its protection. Somewhere out of grove and bog came the elk-cow's soft love call in the twilight, and one early dawn a grouse cock may have offered a laggard and unconvincing invitation from his old mating grounds. There were moments when you seemed to detect a weak echo of spring in the landscape.

Earth and air were all bustling with life. Wasps and ants struggled feverishly to accomplish their last tasks in time, before the frost harried them down into the earth's holes. Southbound flights of birds sailed toward the horizon. The cranes' cry disappeared in the distance, as if swallowed up by the cosmos. You watched life lifting from the crust of the earth and caught yourself, as in all past autumns, experiencing in the rush of wings drawing away a dimension of the freedom that the earthbound pursue but never catch. But you quickly cut the fantasy short by reminding yourself that the birds, whether they navigate by the starry skies or by the earth's magnetism, follow a compulsive pattern imprinted through thousands of bird generations, a remote control out of the depths of the ages.

But now there are no cranes calling from space. The backwash of manifold life, which surged through the landscape, has ebbed out. The ground's tiny creeping things have retreated to their holes. The mushrooms, after a short guest appearance in the light, have been dissolved and have flowed back down into the earth. Hurry and tardy lust have been succeeded by calm and silence.

One frosty night made the foliage brittle. When the

northeast wind struck, the following day, and lifted the trees' colorful hems—the trees sometimes bowing, sometimes rising on tiptoe—the disrobing was quick. Layer after layer was lifted off, a striptease without coquetry, with dignity. Now, on a stroll, you walk upon a carpet of rotting leaves.

The trees around you are your companions. Year after year you have followed their cycle and through them felt nature's rhythm.

Little sticky buds in the time when sap rises. At first you can see them only near-at-hand; at a distance you only suspect them in the lavender haze over the meadows. They drink from the earth's springs, while the soil's covering of frost still shatters with a light metallic tinkling. They capture warmth from the sun, begin to swell, draw themselves together again, swell again. In their still formless softness they conceal the sketch of what shall be a leaf, with its many possibilities. All wrapped up in themselves, the buds contain a fullness of life and warmth. They can withstand unexpectedly frosty nights, even when the column of quicksilver drops a score or more points below freezing. Great power streams through budding trees.

Then the leaves unfold. The formless becomes a multiplicity of forms, each with lobes, points, and fine nets of veins. The metamorphosis goes quickly. You never have time to follow it; every completed leafing-out gives you the feeling of having missed something essential. But from the perianth to the definitive form some of the power has been lost. For the biologists, the loss of warmth is measurable. Perfection means a dimmer, a more damped-down life. All growth involves decline.

After leafing-out: the long period of ripe, static greenness. Almost imperceptibly, the leaves pale till the first rust-specks light their signal lamps. When the days shorten and the sunshine dwindles, operations in the leaves' chlorophyll workshops are gradually shut down. Tannins and other pigments begin to fret the leaves with their glow. When the frost returns, the ability to resist will have dried up. Late in fall, on a hushed morning with mist and frost-glazed grass, a first chill gust of wind takes a tentative tug at the tops of the trees. Several more gusts join in, harder, more purposefully. The change of scene is quick, as quick as once it was at leafing-out.

Leaf fall—how simple and easy it is! A journey in clarity between the invisibilities out of which the tree builds up its life: between the radiation from space that the crown has drunk in and the earth salts that are sucked up through the roots to the heights, and with which the spinning leaves shall be reunited.

Leaf fall is the tree's instalment on its loan from the earth.

You are walking on a carpet of rotting leaves. Walking there surrounded by autumn's balms: odors of the dissolving rain and decay. You are near the earth and you do not try to escape.

You are well acquainted with the seasons' changes in your landscape. You can see the pattern of your own life reflected in that of the leaf. You can see the galaxies' cycle reflected in the leaf's. Your insight tells you of dissolution but not of corruption, of decomposition but not of annihilation. The leaves rustling underfoot are broken down, their cells sink into the soil, become soil. But the cells' powers are indestructible and shall return in new life. Already on the naked branches there are essays toward the buds that the next spring will open.

Thus you can confront the fall: as new life's preparer and intermediary.

A wind that was born someplace beyond the ridges—perhaps in the taiga around Tunguska or over the waters where the albatross hunts—the wind is up to something in the treetops. You can hear it striking a note with its tuning fork and beginning to try out the instrument.

The winds of the globe have two great orchestras to conduct: the waters and the trees. The winds know their instruments, know their possibilities. Man has created his own music, built upon mathematically regulated intervals between air vibrations of different frequencies within the narrow spectrum of sound that man's auditory nerves are able to apprehend. Of notes has man built his loveliest temples. Stroking some hairs from a horse's tail over a piece of twisted sheep gut, man can call forth harmony that lifts him out of himself. But his music is only a reflection of nature's. One who has preserved the ability to listen will be filled with a sense of the timelessness in the symphonies of the winds, the waters, and the woods. Even mightier than now, they rushed over the earth long before man entered upon the scene. They will still resound, more subdued, in diminuendo, long after humankind has made its exit.

Bellowing tubas when avalanches of waves burst against rocky shores. Lullabies crooned by evening's long easy swells. Great forest organs in ponderous fugues. In the meadows, the aspens' nervous zither playing, the oaks' deep cello tones, the birches' rising and falling glissando, as if swept from a hundred violins.

When the wind plays among bare branches, the theme is simple. All embroideries, all embellishments have been scaled away. There is no more to subtract, and nothing needs be added.

This simple, in its atonal beauty, you might imagine the music of the spheres to be.

The stillness over the fields of autumn—the wind only reinforces it.

To listen to stillness is to let yourself be permeated with signals from earth and water, tree and wind. With messages untranslatable into words.

If you tilt your head back to watch the wind playing in the naked treetops, you will discover something the leaf masses hid. Branches stretch out toward the cosmos like roots.

A tree is its own reflection. It draws its life from a double root system: one sucks salts and juices out of the planet's thin layer of soil, the other captures the sun's energy from space. Each system corresponds to the other so harmoniously that you are prepared to play Linnaeus' game: should one turn a tree upside down, the branches ought to take root and find their way down into the earth, while the roots would develop into branches groping toward space.

Of all the expressions of life that evolution has brought forth, trees are the most perfect and complete. They have that solid confidence, that true repose, which proceeds from their having, ages ago, won the survival struggle for light and sun. More clearly than any other, the tree represents the place of all living things between the dust and the cosmos.

The plants of the field are, as a rule, withered by the autumn. Once they have yielded their seed, they have fulfilled their purpose. The leafless tree lives on, summing up the seasons' changes in its form. Its naked architecture, so flexible in its tension, so airy in its weight, gives you a Kantian sense of the thing-in-itself.

Try, yourself, to unleaf your mind, to sweep away all nonessentials. Try to find the same clarified stillness as that of the tree in autumn.

The paths in the autumn meadows are covered by the crumbling leaves. One goes up toward the grove, where the elk's last long, drawn-out love call has died away. You know that path, can find it. Another goes down toward the sea, where the fog is now rising over the cranes' empty stopping place. Neither path is hard to find.

But another may lead inward—toward yourself.

2

> *The lake is in my dream,*
> *the tree is in my blood,*
> *the past is in my bones . . .*
> Kathleen Raine, *On Leaving Ullswater*

THE PATH INWARD—A PATH BACK. Beyond your autumnal wood, beyond all seasons.

    It leads from the familiar into regions that are alien and yet awaken vague feelings that you have been there before. Living things of shifting kinds patter around in the dimness. You sense their shapes, feel their presence almost through your skin; their cries sink into you and open hidden doors to the recognition of affinity. Creatures of your own kind, long dead, glide imperceptibly to your side, their barely audible voices blending with the rustle of the leaves. The deeper you go, the more the shapes are altered, though the transitions are imperceptible. The path winds through trees that become more and more exotic, and over windblown steppes toward a forest far off. It is another forest than your cool autumnal wood, but out of the forgotten long-ago flutter momentary impressions of recognition.

Of the wood thou art.

During our erratic wanderings from the primordial sea to the present, it is true that the wood was only a single phase—but a phase so long and filled with events that it can be considered a beginning for mankind. The Greeks must have felt this intuitively when they had Clio, the muse of history, dwell in a wood. Beneath its verdant arch is found the primordial home of the primates.

Every wood is a series of worlds. Struggling for height, trees create different environments, different living conditions, different possibilities of experience for the many kinds of animal creatures that in their struggle for existence chose the wood as their home and hunting ground. The climbing animals and birds, which keep to the treetops, inhabit a different world from that of the deer moving around in the underbrush, or that of the wood mice gliding across the ground, or that of the worms doing their work in the darkness among the root hairs. Separate worlds—but still in constant relation to one another.

In a distant treetop in the wood of fleeting recognition, you glimpse a primate whose genes have been turned over to you. The distance is too great, your eyes too weak; you can get only an unclear impression of him. A lively, bright-eyed being, not especially big and not without a certain grotesqueness—thus you may, in a few fleeting glimpses, think to apprehend him from your vantage point in time. You look for hints of resemblance, for gestures in which you can see yourself reflected. They ought to be there. But when you try to move closer in order to see him better, he slips off into the green dimness.

Man, avidly seeking, gropes for his roots. He knows that primordial forces work within him. But what are they? Which ones are unchangeable, and which have, in the course of development, been cast off? Why and how did we become what we are? Are we still malleable—can we still be changed?

What are our deepest needs, and what happens if we act contrary to them? What are the real foundations of our values, our experiences of beauty, our goals? Within what limits can we, of our own free will, shape our fate?

There are turning points in the history of thought when an old concept can suddenly be endowed with a tremendous power to illuminate. Such a concept is that of evolution. Even if, earlier, individual visionaries had sensed the continuity of all things and the path of development from simpler to more complex organisms, whenever man tried to find himself he had mostly groped along abysses of fear and mysticism until, in the middle of the nineteenth century, he got on the track of development's principles and driving forces. The concept of evolution has dispersed the thickest haze obscuring our prehistory. Where the darkness remains, evolutionary thought gives a guiding light, the only usable one. It is no longer possible to seek answers to questions of man's nature, acts, and fate without seeing him as part of an evolutionary process.

Among the pioneer researches that prepared the way for the modern concept of evolution was paleontology. It has not yet said its last word. No doubt the earth still contains many answers to our questions. Some have been answered only in the most recent decades. Exhumed skulls and other bits of bone are not so lifeless as some historians seem to imagine. Rather plainly, they can tell about primitive dwellings, weapons and tools, about hunting and the species hunted, about dangers, and about troop cohesion among primates who lived millions of years ago. They allow us to follow tolerably well the gradual transformation of a tree-climbing primate into a man. The missing links have lately become somewhat fewer.

To begin with, the trashy multitude of species names has been tidied up, a multitude that resulted from the ambition to give a new designation to every discovery of a skull or a jaw fragment that differed from what had earlier been brought to light. Evolution has many strings to its bow. We do not know all of them yet. However, we now know that, during explosive evolutionary phases, when a species spreads over new territories (with all that that implies about a need to adjust to new environments) individual variations can be very great. The genetic inheritance contains dormant qualities that can be released under pressure of shifting surroundings. Understanding this, it has now been agreed that the different types of manlike beings that moved through the ancient world some half a million years ago will be brought together into a single species, *Homo erectus*—the upright walking man, nearest ancestor of our own kind.

But evolution also has a clear tendency to split the species, to bet on different possibilities. It was probably this tendency that complicated things for the paleontologists. It is simply one of the basic features of the way evolution works, a feature that gives rise to different tribes, different races, gradually different species. The late Neanderthals who, resignedly, sought refuge in Europe's caves during the last ice age, died out; they had ended up in one of evolution's blind alleys. The earlier members of the Neanderthaloid family were slenderer, more like modern man. From them our stubborn race reckons its origin, as did our clumsier, doomed cousins.

The excited probing into Africa's soil that has been going on in recent decades is now beginning to turn up new leads to the nearest predecessor of *Homo erectus*. Beings hidden in the earth for a million years or so rose up again in the finds made by the long-misjudged Raymond Dart on the edge of the Kalahari Desert and by the untiring Dr. and Mrs. Louis B. Leakey at Olduvai in Tanzania. Once again grinning up at the African sun, they showed an interesting anatomical mixture of features pointing toward man and of features somewhere halfway toward the higher apes. The former predominated. The ankle bone, the inclination of the pelvis, the bearing of backbone and skull tell of upright walking, but the kneecap leads us to suspect that the walk was always somewhat swaying. The brain volume was small, however, and the jaws were large. *Australopithecus,* which came to be the unifying designation for these half-men, had a more robust type and a more graceful one. As late as a couple of years ago it seemed reasonable to suppose that evolution had worked with the more graceful type, while the other one, like the late Neanderthals, had disappeared down some side track.

New finds in Kenya and Ethiopia are now changing the picture. A research team led by Dr. and Mrs. Leakey's son, Richard Leakey (who is suddenly as famous as they), has found the remains of a manlike primate who lived on the windswept savannahs some two and a half to three million years ago. His brain volume was greater than that of the specimens hitherto collected under the name *Australopithecus.* His walk seems to have been upright, and the site where his remains were found reveals that he could fashion the simpler sort of tools out of stone. These new finds open interesting perspectives into the past. They demonstrate that manlike beings existed some millions of years earlier than we had hitherto supposed. They can also be interpreted to show that the line of human development has been somewhat different from that along which Dart and the elder Leakeys had led us only recently.

With increased if not complete assurance, we are able to follow our species a little distance back through time. But we have still hardly stepped outside our own neighborhood.

The path winds further, becomes more tangled. Some way along it, we see, dimly, a fine-boned creature, *Ramapithecus.* Several things about him suggest that he may have been a forerunner of man. Ten to fifteen million years ago he ranged all the way from East Africa to East Asia. Cautiously, the paleontologists are satisfied with hinting that a two-legged walk ought to have made dispersion over such great distances easier. Behind him, in turn, moves a jumping tree-spirit, *Dryopithecus,* an ape that seems—if the fossil finds have been interpreted correctly—to have climbed in the tree at times, to have scampered on the ground at other times.

Thus far, we can follow a fossil pattern, albeit one with some missing connections. We visualize an ape who leaves the tree existence and see how he slowly raises himself and how his brain volume is increased. The paleontologist has helped a bit along the way. But when we ask ourselves what images moved within the frontal lobes and influenced the individual's and the species' reactions and behavior, the empty skulls grin at us mutely.

The young and vital branch of research called ethology ought to be able to dispel much of the silence. It finds itself in the favorable position of having almost everything undone, mistakes as well as discoveries. It attempts to chart the behavior patterns that tie living things together and to explore why behavior is as it is.

Obviously, the closer species stand to one another, the greater are the similarities in their behavior. Nowadays every student of elementary biology and anthropology is taught the similarities between man and his tardily acknowledged third cousins, the higher apes, in anatomy, gestures, mimicry, and desire to experiment. Maybe he also knows that man, gorilla, and chimpanzee have the same blood group series and similar chromosome patterns. He knows, too, why the likenesses are there. Ethology goes further and tries to explore the deeper impelling forces.

Now that ethologists are finding their way out of the zoos and into the fresh air, out onto the savannahs and into the forests, they are encountering a world whose signs could not have been made intelligible before the insights of evolution began to direct our thinking. The study of the species that stand nearest to us ought to teach us much about ourselves. We should not forget, however, what some excited investigators seem to have forgotten, that we are dealing here with relatives whose development has forced each into its own narrow ecological niche, constraining each to rigid specialization. No group, tribe, or species can have descended from any now living, but each has, instead, some predecessor that it shares with other groups, tribes, or species now living. What you are seeking, ultimately, is the creature who climbed in the treetops before the family tree had yet divided.

Several researchers suspect that this creature must have been less specialized than the modern higher ape. It cannot be a coincidence that the foetuses of higher apes are more similar to grown men than to grown apes. Much seems to point toward evolution having excelled, someplace in our common background, in a principle to which we give the unlovely name of paedomorphosis. This signifies that development takes a step backward from the highly specialized and fixed to a rawer and more primitive starting point (with its still unexploited possibilities), as if to get a running start for a leap forward.

Here comes paleontology again with serviceable hints, even if they now become more vague. It shows us a little fellow, *Parapithecus,* whose fossil was found in Egyptian deposits that ought to be thirty to forty million years old. No pharaoh can compare in importance with this little creature; no pyramid can be nearly as interesting as the place of its finding. What paleontologists think they have found here is a transitional form from lower to higher primates, an unspecialized half-ape from which both lower and higher apes, among them man himself, may possibly trace their ancestry. It shows striking likenesses to the tarsioids, of which a single genus still lives in the jungles of the Philippines, the Celebes, Borneo, and Sumatra, where it seems to regard recent intruders with an age-old surprise in its great eyes.

A tarsioid species that became extinct earlier is presumed to have had a place in the family tree of the higher primates.

Perhaps one can find another hint in the sanctuary for the living past that Madagascar represents. Sometime in the beginning of the Tertiary Epoch, as geologists explain it, this island must have broken off from the African mainland and glided out to sea, thereby separating a fragment of the epoch's animal world from the mainland. As the reptile age reached its end on the continent, mammals specialized for various ecosystems entered the picture: lions and leopards began to roar, apes stepped into the developmental panorama. Existence became more and more varied and filled with dangers, and natural selection became more rigorous. But not an echo of this noisy rough-and-tumble reached the sheltered island. It became a reservation for its original mammals, which had none but each other to compete with. In its lush forests evolution had no need to hurry. The first, disruptive human beings did not reach the island until around the beginning of the Christian era.

Later, the island would be scalped after all. The day was past when the law required that a man who did violence to a tree should be decapitated upon its stump. But in the woods that remain one can look back, as if through a powerful telescope, some fifty to sixty million years in time, back into a world of half-apes, *Lemuridae*. Judging by fossil finds on the mainland, these creatures are rather like the ones that accompanied the island out to sea. If millions of years have rolled by without making any greater impression on the lemurides' bodies than this, one may suspect that behavior patterns have been conserved as well. Perhaps this gives us a unique possibility of looking back into the dawn of the primates.

There in the greenery move rare creatures with big eyes that retain even now some of the reptile age's cold watchfulness, with a protruding nose like a lingering memory of a ground-level existence ages ago, with a brain smaller than the apes', but with supple climbing ability, long sensitive fingers, and lively movements.

The French ethologist Jean-Jacques Petter has made some preliminary studies in the lemurs' woods. He has found that the more developed species live in well-integrated communities, in clans or embryonic nations, some of whose members guard the group's territory so that others can develop parental care and gentleness. The lemurs have not yielded up their secrets yet—not by any means. It should be an international responsibility to create effective protection for this fragment of the Tertiary Epoch, which may conceal the answers to several of man's questions.

Some species of *Lemuridae* have, like man, forty-six chromosomes; the higher apes have forty-eight. If that amounts to evidence that they are our close relatives, it is not man, in any case, who needs to be ashamed of the relationship.

Thus, in the thickets of fleeting recognition, you seem to be glimpsing the shape of that creature whose genes have found their way down through millions of years to you. Still you cannot catch him. As soon as you try, he slips away. Nor can you be sure what or who took him up into the trees. Once we tended to guess at a tree-climbing fish that no longer felt at home in the pools along the beach. Nowadays we believe it was a shrew-like form that was being bested in the struggle for ground life's food supplies and so went looking for a new ecosystem.

However, what you can really be quite sure of—and the certitude gives you something important—is that tree life turned into one of the decisive stages in becoming human. We had to get up in the trees, if we were ever going to be able to come back down as man.

The early primates' physique and senses must have been adapted by evolution to life in the tree. Natural selection favored the most skillful climbers, elite gymnasts on primeval bars and beam, those who could reach the most inaccessible fruits. Hands and feet developed into grasping tools suited to clambering along tree trunks and swinging from branch to branch.

But the primate who swung himself between the branches needed something more than a strong grasping hand to be able to estimate distances and possibilities. Ground level is naturally a world of odors, where one noses out one's food. For the mammal at the treetop level, with its complicated patterns, the sense of sight became the most important for survival. To throw oneself from branch to branch demands keen sight and precision. The shrunken, flattened nose and the forward-oriented eyes, which made stereoscopic vision possible, were some of tree life's gifts to the primate.

All this must have been highly significant for the development of the brain. The eye's fixation upon distances and goals, the judgment of possibilities, the grasping hand that had to close itself at just the right moment, all this complicated operation required a coordination of the central nervous system. This, in turn, created the keen sense of dimension that is basic to all of man's civilization. Konrad Lorenz, the founder of ethology, has offered convincing evidence that only tree-climbers can solve spatial problems, and he finds in this the probable basis for our most complicated cognitive operations.

So far, the prospects must have been the same for the different branches that were slowly beginning to push out from the common family tree. In the leaf-dappled tree existence, however, development could only proceed to a certain limit. Tree life had created certain possibilities, but for these to be realized another change of environment was required.

The primate that would become man lived in intimate harmony with the trees, whose fruits nourished him. He lived nearer to the birds and the sky than the animals on the ground did. The wind's rustling in the leaves sank into him; it would make a lasting impression on his emotional life. But if he were ever to develop into man, he would have to go down to the ground again.

Why did he not remain in his Eden? Why did he, fifteen to twenty million years ago, break out of the leaf-dappled existence? The reasons can be reconstructed with some certainty. The mild and luxuriant Miocene ebbed slowly out and was followed by the Pliocene's drouth. The ice ages swept their chilly mantles back and forth over the northern hemisphere and brought with them radical changes in living conditions, even in the tropics. A harsher climate thinned out the tropical forests. It got very crowded around the shrinking food supply.

Perhaps the primate with the seed of man within him had been driven away from his declining food supply by creatures even more agile than he. Perhaps he had for some time been on his way toward the lower branches, where the gorilla stayed put. To survive, he had to try new food resources. He became a meat eater, and the hunting of meat led him, finally, to a life on the ground.

Not of free will but under pressure of necessity he left the trees' sheltered environment. Almost in the Old Testament sense, he was driven out of the Garden.

Maybe he tried as best he could to hang onto his accustomed environment. Wilfred Le Gros Clark, one of today's leading evolutionists, has proposed the seemingly paradoxical idea that the new ground existence did not come about through the primate's giving up tree life. As the woods dwindled, he had to find his way across ever wider expanses of grassland to get from one clump of trees to another. But everywhere in the groves the pantries were getting barer, and what resources he did find probably had their more agile exploiters and their angry defenders. Bit by bit he was simply forced to go over to a life in the open.

In this new life, the arboreal creature, driven from

its natural home, had to compete with beasts of prey that had been formed for hunting on the ground. In the treetops the external dangers had been few, the possibilities of flight, many; in the open the primate was ill-equipped for the survival struggle. In a peculiar but logical interplay, the hunting and the hunted affect each others' development: the quickest prey have the best chance to escape, the most cunning and best-armed predator has the best chance to catch its prey. Evolution allows those that are best suited to escape or attack to spread their genes further. In this way the different species are honed to a fine edge. The primate with the seed of man within him possessed neither the other prey's quickness nor the other predators' attack- and defense-weapons: saber-teeth, horns, claws.

Not nimble enough for the wood, not quick or protected enough for the ground—no longer quite at home anywhere: his adventure should reasonably have ended in one of the blind alleys where so many other species had been extinguished.

Obviously, just this paradox provided the occasion for a new and definitive step toward the primate's becoming man. Maybe it was precisely at this stage that the first rough sketch of our towers of Babel, our hydrogen bombs, and our space ships took shape.

Out of the tree existence the emigrant had taken a many-sided heritage that could be developed further.

The plant world and the animal world have different orientations. Almost without exception trees and plants, which are life's primary manifestations and the mediators in the interplay between the sun's energy and the ground's acids and salts, strive upward. Their basic orientation is vertical. Animals, the secondary manifestations of life, which live upon the plants' liberated oxygen and, directly or indirectly, upon their stored resources of nourishment, are horizontal in their basic orientation. Their muzzles, noses, and snouts hang down toward the ground, their gaze seeks the earth.

However, some primates must have acquired a half-erect posture quite early. The architecture of the trees invited one to assume sitting positions. Acrobatics in the branches gave the body elasticity. On the ground it became natural to move with light support from the knuckles of the forward extremities. The hands were grasping tools and not so well suited to four-footed gait as the paws and hooves of other mammals. It was a kind of halfway point, some degrees away from the basic horizontal theme; the trend to upright posture was there.

This trend the creature driven out of its garden could and had to develop further; it became a necessity for his survival. As his movements became gradually adapted to the new scheme, his rear extremities gradually lost their ability to grasp. The foot was flattened to the shape of a sole, and its rear part was reconstructed into a heel, which gave steadiness and balance to the upright posture. In the heel and the sole lay concealed the possibilities of wandering.

In his uprightness the primate copied, in a special way, the trees from which he had come. He became the animal kingdom's only vertical type—a mammal with the tree's posture. When, in a daring aphorism, the Spanish philosopher of culture Salvador de Madariaga spoke of man as "a tree that has packed up its earth and got moving," it was no new vision. In Nordic myth the first people were Ash and Elm. The Sioux Indians told a similar tale. Insight and wisdom lay concealed within these myths.

Upright carriage also made it biologically possible for the primate to develop other abilities that his tree period had called forth. When his front extremities were no longer needed for locomotion, the grasping ability he had practiced in the branches could be applied to the making of tools and weapons, clumsy at first, then gradually more and more refined. This laid the technological foundation for the coming human civilization.

The mental foundations were laid through the great

brain. It had been developed as a tendency out of the patterns of movement that life in the treetops had shown to be most practical. What the wood had foreshadowed, life in the open could fully develop. A larger brain is a costly luxury. In a four-footed gait, it would have hung toward the ground. It demands a large forehead, lifted above the shoulders by a column of muscles. Two-leggedness was the great brain's biological precondition. The survival struggle in the open, with its shifting situations and harsh demands, probably provided the environmental precondition. The weapon, necessary to meet the dangers of open country, probably also stimulated development toward a larger brain—a process opposite to what has earlier been believed. In a new and unprotected environment, the great brain became the primate's answer to the other predators' tusks and horns.

The upright posture, the weapon, and the brain were the armament that made survival possible.

Every newborn child, the most helpless in creation, reminds us of how recent these triumphs are. During its development within the mother, the human foetus repeats the process of evolution from a single-cell organism in the primordial ocean onward, with the gills of the fish, the yolk-sac of the reptile, and the tail and hairiness of the mammal as visible memories of development. But the last lessons in evolution's book are first repeated after birth.

The hands of a newborn baby have an unexpected strength. If you offer the baby a finger or an object, you are surprised by its tight grip. If you let a newborn grasp a rope, it can hang upon it and hold up its own weight. If you let it cling tightly to the rope with both hands and feet, it hangs there like a sloth. The baby seems to have begun life with a biological memory from the treetop days.

It is still a long time before the baby can raise itself, stand, and walk on steady feet. This is a reminder that two-leggedness is so new that our anatomy hasn't yet become entirely adapted to it. The newborn baby's head cannot be held up without support; the brain is too big, before the muscle column to carry it is developed. The chimpanzee is far ahead of the human baby in handling tools, right up to the stage when the great brain's activities awaken; but when that does happen, the baby's development proceeds quickly.

The hunting pack was a setting in which the primate's brain volume tripled within a short time. One is led to believe that the pack, too, was a precondition for the awakening of dormant possibilities. Through group cooperation men could join their powers and experience in the pursuit of food and meet the risks of the new life together.

Yet out of the dangers and out of the groups something else grew up, too.

Nowadays we know what Darwin seems to have suspected but never succeeded in expressing: that practically all animals are territorial species. The territory guarantees food. Whether group- or pair-territory is involved, individuals unite in the defense of their own turf, their own territory. Outwardly, solidarity; inwardly, demands for identity, living-space, individual distance: this applies equally to apes at eating- or resting-places and to swallows perching on a telephone wire. The more observations ethologists collect, the clearer the outlines of a universal law of territorial behavior in which the variations are admittedly great but whose exceptions only serve to remind us of the rule itself.

Defending a territory gives the defender confidence and strength. Conversely, the intruder feels all the less confident, all the more "conscious of guilt," the more he advances into the other's territory. If there is a fight, the defender wins practically every time. Most often, however, animals respect each others' territories and are satisfied to work off their aggressive tendencies through ritualized behavior: rowdiness, threatening gestures, and other exciting actions performed right at the border. But even if the encounter should reach the point of combat, evolution has imprinted powerful inhibitions (especially in the higher vertebrates) against inflicting an injury on one's own kind. The inferior one submits by taking positions that expose the most vulnerable parts of the body to the enemy. A chimpanzee stretches out its vulnerable hand. A wolf lays itself flat on the ground, baring its jugular vein. A raven offers its eye, so easy for another raven's beak to peck out. The stronger never makes use of this opportunity; he is satisfied to have established his superiority. In a wonderful way, this pattern, imprinted through the ages, has the effect of protecting the species.

It must have been just this delicately woven pattern that the primate with the seed of man within him followed when living in the trees. When he stepped down to the ground the pattern was ripped asunder. His new way of life had to be purchased at the cost of the support and security that a rigid habit gives.

In the strange ground environment he became a restless seeker, one lacking a firm mooring in the naturalness of fixed ways. As a meat eater, he had to seek out his quarry across vast domains, and he had to investigate other animals' habits. The fierce competition with creatures long established on the ground forced him to adapt himself to different surroundings and thereby trained him to versatility. While the various forest apes were driven to specialize, each within its narrowly delimited biotype, emerging man developed into what Konrad Lorenz has strikingly characterized as "a specialist in nonspecialization." This adventurous life, rich in shifting situations, provoked the curious probing and examining, the appetite for the unknown, that would come to distinguish man from other species. Inquisitiveness, the lust to examine, became one of the primate's gifts to his descendants.

But there was also a darker gift, one that would come to separate man from most other species. Many times when hunting bands met, acts of submission may have taken place, of which memories remain in man's kneeling and his bowing of the head. But somewhere on a wind-tossed savannah the inhibitions against harming others of one's own species were blown away. Man-in-the-making became—with consequences that extend into our own time and threaten our own future—one of the few creatures in nature that do not draw back from killing others of their own kind.

What went wrong?

Ethologists and their preachment-prone explicators dispute this question, dispute with a hot-headedness that seems in itself to exemplify man's inherent tendency toward aggression. One school, the pessimistic one, holds that the tendency is as strong a drive, in individuals' and species' struggle to survive, as the drive to reproduce. It is one with territorial behavior, being found among ants and rats, fighting fish and gray geese. Ethologists who study apes in captivity have reported tensions and brutality, torture and murder. From such observations, the conclusion has been drawn that the aggressive tendency is deeply and ineradicably engraved in man, as an inheritance from earlier lives.

Another school, more optimistic, expresses itself vigorously against that opinion and holds emphatically that "war is not in our genes." Aggressiveness, they say, is not inherited but is something learned in our culture. They point out how bloodless—almost without exception—territorial behavior is.

They criticize the practice of drawing conclusions from how animals behave in laboratories and zoos. Animals in captivity are exposed to stresses, especially crowding, that break down the normal pattern of coexistence, cause ulcers and shock, and let trouble loose. Observing the life of wild apes, the field researcher can get an entirely different picture. Apes in the wild often live in troops similar in size to primitive human tribal societies—and similar, for that matter, to the youth-gangs in modern big cities. The troop's organization is stable, closed, like a nation, hierarchically organized, with a leadership apparatus and a president who may top an enlightened despotism or a patriarchal democracy. Within the troop, calm and order; between the troops, peaceful coexistence. When two groups meet, it is the leaders' assignment to judge their relative strengths. Guided by an astute leader, the weaker group gives way. Among certain apes, troops can make tribal alliances, superpowers. Aggressive apes are never appointed to lead; the troop prefers experience, wisdom, cautiousness. The higher apes are, in reality, decidedly peaceful. Herein lies, according to one writer, a message of hope for their human relatives.

Quietly, the layman wonders whether it is possible that the most eager combatants on each side of this ethological quarrel are overemphasizing certain aspects and suppressing others. When animals in their natural surroundings are content to hold their territories only by howling and making threatening gestures, surely they are building upon dearly bought experience, somewhere in the past, of what best preserves the species. Such ritualized behavior cannot have arisen of itself. The origins of the ritual must have been in real struggles, perhaps at a stage in evolution when the territorial pattern had not yet found its fixed form in nature and in instinct. If such is the case, then, despite all subsequent inhibitions, the aggressive tendency is sleeping somewhere, ready to be waked if the usual living pattern breaks down.

This is precisely what happens when animals are under stress. When the primate who had human potential stepped down from the tree, the situation he faced must have been enormously stressful. The ground environment was truly hostile—lacking in shelter, insecure, filled with dangers that must have been formidable. The Australopithecines whose remains were found in some caves in the Transvaal can tell us something of the dangers still encountered millions of years after the descent from the tree. The researcher who analyzed the finds explains that they could hardly have had their living quarters in the caves. No other remains point to such a practice, and, in the caves' darkness, at a time before they had fire or knew how to frighten other animals away with it, they would have been vulnerable to other predators. The researcher concluded that they must have been dragged there by other predacious animals.

Life in such an environment must have meant a tension in no way less than what animals experience in a zoo. Furthermore, in the wild there is another factor that can break down the most stable group and territory patterns and the most firmly established forms of peaceful coexistence: overpopulation in relation to food supply. During the rain-poor, windblown millions of years that followed the Miocene Era, the newcomer on the ground must have been thrown into a life-and-death competition with his own kind for the scarce food resources. All this could explain why a peaceful tree-ape became an aggressive ground creature.

There are recent examples from the human community that would support such a guess. With deep personal engagement, an American anthropologist, Colin M. Turnbull, has studied an African hunting and gathering people, the Ik, who live in a region where Uganda, Kenya, and Sudan intersect. Until quite recently the people of this tribe lived in a solid and well-developed social structure, in harmony with their surroundings and with themselves. However, not long ago events confined them to a mere corner of their ancient hunting lands, where there existed neither enough game to hunt nor enough fruit to gather. This led to a quick and total dissolution of all tribal and familial ties, to a collapse of the entire social organization. The individual Ik was cast into a frightful isolation, each and every one intent only on trying to snatch to himself whatever he could of the meager food supply—without any consideration for spouse, children, parents, or others. In the most lethal sense, each man's loss was another's gain.

Despite such examples, some people console themselves with the idea that only learned social patterns, not a hereditary taint, cause disintegrative, aggressive behavior whether of animals or of men. Maybe they are right, maybe not. Nothing can be established, everything must be supposed. But unfortunately their reasoning does not seem completely convincing. Modern genetics appears to be on the way to breaking down the traditional boundary between heredity and environment, between the inborn and the acquired in our behavior. Evidently the lessons of long-standing habit can be worn into the genes. We cannot exclude the possibility that aggressiveness has come, in some active way, to thrust itself into the process of natural selection.

Natural selection arranges things in such a way that those individuals who are best equipped and most useful for the continuance of the species get the greatest chance to survive and reproduce themselves. A time must have come in the struggle for leadership and the favors of the females when brain took a decided lead over mere brawn. Those males who took best advantage of the brain's potential got a better chance to spread their genes further through the race. This, in turn, could account for the great brain's quick development.

But in the rivalry between hunting bands, pugnacity, bravery, and fighting ability must also have seemed valuable, improving each band's chances of maintaining itself. To say that the peaceful ape society in a relatively stable situation never chooses aggressive leaders would hardly be relevant. In a life of hard and permanent pressure, the "warlike virtues" may have come to be highly favored by natural selection within the species.

The combination of intelligence and aggressiveness may ultimately explain the success of a species that, after being driven from the Garden, seemed to have most of the odds against it. But this was at the same time the riskiest alloy that evolution had ever made in its crucible.

Clio remained in the wood.

For the low-browed Abel, who slowly began to seek out more and more distant hunting grounds, the open country became, after all, no more than a part of his environment. The wood and its life remained his familiars. Even if his hunting base was situated at a river mouth or by the seashore, he had to go into the wood again and again to pursue his quarry. His old home in the treetops was closed to him, but in case of need he could make use of his never entirely forgotten skill of climbing to seek protection and food in the trees.

Gradually the hunting primate was transformed into the human hunter who would spread his kind over Terra in continual wandering, seeking, over hundreds of thousands of years. The sole and heel made this long wandering possible, while the great brain's increasing ability to find combinations and solutions eased the adaptations to new environments.

During this continual wandering, the wood was always there as a background, as a shady roof for his dwelling, as a hunting ground. There is in nature a secret accord between the hunter and the hunted. The hunter lived within the same physical surroundings as his quarry and was subject to the same biological laws.

The wind's gambols over the water and through the treetops filled his ears and stayed with him in the days' ramblings and the nights' embraces. He was a part of the forest's life, instinctively knowing its ways and reading its signs.

Even after Cain had begun to sow his grain and tame his animal food, Abel continued to wander over the land. Still, it was Cain, the husbandman and village founder, who, with an even newer way of life, finally got the upper hand. What symbolism there is in the biblical story, that this change could not take place without violence! So long as the ground was only cultivated, man still lived, it's true, near nature's creative powers. But when these powers were put in shackles of asphalt and concrete, something fundamental in our living conditions was changed. Something was stoned—to death?—when man broke with his original natural context.

In a new way of life, created by his own technology but with millions of years' impressions and feelings from his forest existence invisibly imprinted in his emotional life, reflex patterns, and biological needs, man has again ended up not really belonging anywhere—has landed in a homelessness and insecurity perhaps even deeper than what earlier confronted the unsheltered primate, driven from the treetops down to the ground.

There have nearly always been a number of knotted contradictions in man's relation to his original environment. They cannot be captured in any simple formula about love of the tree, fear of the woods. Love of the tree is simple enough, but where the woods are concerned fear and attraction are twin brothers.

You seek a child who had your name, you try to follow him on his first rambles in a wood. You want to regain the feelings, impressions and experiences that streamed through the barefoot lad. What you capture is a fragment; you cannot relive the intensity of the experience. Besides, much of it was probably different from what a deceitful memory tells you it was. You and the lad are the same, and yet not quite the same, individual.

Even so, you can still sense the strong odor of pine resin and labrador tea. You recognize the coarse softness of the moss under your naked feet and know the dry needles and branches of the path. You are amazed at the snail's shining blackness and startled when a wood-bird bursts up out of the silence on heavy wing beats. What lurks farther on, beyond the bones of the dead tree, past the moss-covered boulder, over the next ridge? You know you're not allowed, you dread the unknown a little, but you feel that you must. You are drawn deeper into the wood despite your heart's beating a little more audibly than usual—or maybe just because it does. Something is holding you back; something stronger is drawing you on.

Or autumnal evenings when the wood was filled with strange sounds—crunching in the brush and rustling in the branches, long-drawn-out calls and cries—sounds magnified by the darkness and your imagination. The lad had no real fear of the dark! But he had a dark, excitement-filled impression of life that was there and yet could not be seen.

Perhaps the child's reactions and feelings were not so different from those of the primitive hunter. The wood was his source of food and he had to know its possibilities. His appetite for the unknown combined with the pressure of necessity, continually luring him toward new domains. But the wood also contained dangers known and unknown. His intuitions of the realities of the wood were interlaced with experiences of mysterious powers, some of them good, others to be avoided or else appeased, if possible.

The trees lived on in man's imaginings. They took a central place in mankind's earliest myths. Dryads lived in hollow trunks, and fairies tiptoed in the shadows. The oaks of Dodona rustled, and the tree of knowledge tempted us with its fruits. Beings half animal, half man were glimpsed behind the tree trunks. Trees became the dwelling places of the spirits of the departed or, themselves, mystic life-giving beings. Mighty tree-patriarchs launched men's imagination toward visions of world-trees that bore up creation or were creation itself.

That most powerful of myths: the Nordic one about Yggdrasil, the world ash-tree, whose roots embraced the earth and whose branches joined the vault of heaven.

Utilitarian ages, which often had little insight into true usefulness, practical centuries, which all too easily confused practicality with quick profit, assailed the planet's woods. Great stands of forest were burned, felled, and uprooted to make room for man's grain and goats, until nothing remained to bind and renew the soil. As a consequence, entire civilizations were washed down clear-cut slopes, to disappear in whirling dust storms. Out of the forest charcoal was fetched for the iron smelter, and timbers for the ship; the wood gave sword and armor, and carried the traders, conquistadors, and plunderers to distant countries and continents—until man one day found that the extortion had gone so far that there began to be shortages in the real treasury. To a great extent, the history of the rise and fall of the great powers could be written as a chronicle of man's relations with the forests.

As his distance from the woods increased, man became more and more a stranger in the forest world. However, he could not tear up his own roots as easily as he could those of the trees. Despite increasing remoteness, and amidst a supposed practicality, the wood has kept its dark hold over its former denizen. To plant a tree has been one of man's significant acts. Doesn't the real wisdom of life consist in planting a tree today, even if you know you are to die in the morning?

When you perform that act, which sometimes seems to have an almost ritual character, it is as if the swelling power of the tree imparted some of its mystery to you. An old tree reminds us of our life's brevity and at the same time mysteriously links us to past and coming generations.

There stands the venerable tree that guards our house! Under its branches, great-grandfather said goodbye, going to a war from which he never returned. There, in a shy moment, grandfather gave grandmother an engagement ring. In its shade, after his day's work, father used to immerse himself in one of his well-worn favorite books. The newly planted tree: will it carry some message onward to the coming generations?

When we wish to give a little perspective to our fleeting individual lives, we usually look at ourselves as branches on a family tree with trunk and roots in past generations and with promises of new branching-out in generations to come.

The annual rings of a very old tree give an odd depth to history, making much of what impresses us as essential seem ephemeral. Yew trees have been found in Europe that are thought to be three thousand years of age. Their annual rings encompass most of our known history. A few rings back, Napoleon is brought to St. Helena; a few rings further back, Columbus stands off from Palos; there, at a millimeter-thin annual ring, our time reckoning begins; and there, six narrow annual rings tell of the Trojan War.

Under the dark branches, bands of wandering Goths may have lit their watchfires and Roman legionaries watered their horses. When the tree was just beginning to sprout, Europe was going unevenly over from the stone age to the bronze age. Perhaps, once, a hunter clad in skins stood near the young sapling and looked around for his quarry.

When boys climb in a tree they are utilizing our race's never-quite-forgotten climbing ability. Up there in the treetops they can turn themselves into Tarzan or Robin Hood or Hawkeye. Or the branches can be a crow's nest for keeping watch on the voyage to the New World. Games like other games—but, with their fresh immediacy, boys in a tree unreflectingly express something that is preserved beneath the surface layer of consciousness as a biological memory. In the grown-up observer who has not altogether turned to stone, the memory manifests itself as a sting of loss.

Trees have followed us through long wandering. They refuse to let us go even when we shut ourselves up behind concrete and glass. In the deepest cranny of the back of the brain, a secret tree-longing is sighing—the heritage of *Ramapithecus, Dryopithecus, Parapithecus.*

Of the wood thou art . . .

3

No words but the right words,
The ones that have crowns, and bird songs in them,
Give shade as the trees give shade.
Hjalmar Gullberg

IN THE BEGINNING, the word was not.

How difficult for civilized man to imagine a wordless existence! All our imaginings are made of words and are clothed in them. We think in words. Human society in all its ramifications functions through words. They are the building blocks of civilization.

In purely physical terms words are nothing but used-up air forced through windpipe and larynx and kneaded by tongue, teeth, and lips. And yet they reflect everything touching man and his life.

In the beginning the brain was a cavity of wordless sensations. Words must have been conceived somewhere in the transition between manlike ape and apelike man. The way back to the word-cradle is tangled to the point of impenetrability. Linguists fumble, having to depend on theories and suppositions.

All animals seem to have an inborn instinct to communicate with others of their kind, an instinct that is an expression of their urge to live. How it is expressed varies with the biological preconditions of each. In nature's point-counterpoint, each species has its own system of signals, whose content is sometimes grasped and understood by other species.

To signal that danger threatens, the beaver slaps his tail on the water, the roebuck stamps on the ground. The female elk's long-drawn-out melodic "oaa oaa" tells the bull that she is ready to accept him. A male butterfly and a female can, by radar signals insensible to us, make contact with each other right through a great city's traffic noise and guide each other to a rendezvous. The dance that bees perform at the honeycomb tells of the discovery of a new field for honey gathering so-and-so far away in this-or-that direction. In springtime, the thrush's trills give warning: This is my territory, stay out!

The instinctive signals serve the primitive life functions. The more highly developed a species becomes, the more strongly an aspect of consciousness appears in the attempt to get attention.

With several primates, such as gibbons and howler monkeys, we have been able to distinguish dozens of different cries and sounds and to explain their significance. These vocalizations are complemented by gestures that range from threat to tenderness. Here, perhaps, one may refer to "attempts at speech." With porpoises, regarded by man as the world's most intelligent creatures next to himself, we find a rich variety of expressive forms.

The primate in the wood of fleeting recognition—you cannot catch his distinctive sound any more than you can get a clear picture of his features. Yet you seem to hear across millions of years the feeble echo of an echo of an echo of grunting, howling, mumbling. You interpret them as expressions of fear and threat, hunger and sexual craving, well-being and suffering.

The echo is within ourselves.

Pondering a newborn baby's means of expression, you seem to find the same recapitulation of mankind's past that you saw manifested on the biological plane: a gradual development from instinctive cries of pain and hunger and chuckles of well-being toward more deliberate attempts by this budding awareness to make contact.

Even in grown-ups, rudiments of the prehuman can suddenly be bared. In unexpected situations, in violent fright or in an attack of blinding rage, words fail us. Through all the layers of words, the primate's cry forces its way out of our throats. Pain seeks expression in moans and groans. Many of our gestures are mechanical, already imprinted in us in the childhood of the species. In anger, we bare our teeth as if to bite.

Shouts and cries are expressions of moods and feelings. They designate nothing, describe nothing. The transition from expressive cries to words, which could designate and describe, has been regarded as the real threshold of becoming man. It is just that process which is so hard to recapture. Comparison with other species, obviously, no longer gives us much help.

Anatomy can testify to the biological basis of the transition. Even here, man's upright posture was the key. The long neck that carried the head and the inward-curving nape created the prerequisites for a collaboration between different muscles in bringing about a greater variation of sound. Just as weapon- and tool-making required coordination of eye, brain, and hand, speech required a fine coordination of the cerebral nerves and the muscles and organs close to the brain. The growing brain contained latent possibilities of developing speech, while speech probably became, in turn, the last in a series of cooperating forces that came to develop the brain.

Even so, the act of creation itself remains a riddle. When did it happen, and in what way?

A modern school of linguistic researchers, whose authoritative spokesman is Noam Chomsky, points out that investigating the nature of speech is of central importance to investigating human nature. Surely they are right. Chomsky doubts, however, that the development of speech would have followed the same processes as biological evolution. He cannot see anything that ties together "lower" and "higher" stages of speech and, therefore, he finds no reason to suspect that any evolution has taken place between the different stages. Instead he casts a furtive glance toward principles as yet unknown, principles that may develop only at the higher levels of organization. Just when that higher level of organization might have been reached by our species is a matter upon which Chomsky himself has apparently not expressed himself. Others, however, have wanted to situate the beginning of speech only a few tens of thousands of years back in time. This would mean that the different languages would have sprung up with a striking simultaneity, within different societies, as a result of principles previously implanted in man.

The scientific layman finds it difficult to be convinced by this almost metaphysical argumentation. All expertise runs the risk of losing sight of simplicity and wholeness in the thicket of details. Despite the architectural differences among the three thousand or more human languages, there nevertheless seem to be certain primary features pointing toward a possible common origin. If you consider it probable that there was a connection between the development of the brain and the development of speech, perhaps you have to look for the source of speech several hundred thousand years back.

The group cooperation that a new and risk-filled way of life required, after the primate came down from the tree, ought gradually to have made new means of expression necessary. The hunting group must have developed a system of gestures and sounds, certainly inarticulate, but providing a necessary prelude to the development of articulated words. For the cooperating group, the instinctive cries of pain and hunger and chuckles of well-being—the feeling-language— were not sufficient. They had to find their way to some elementary designations. Of all the attempts to answer the question "In what way?," the most seductive theory is the one first enunciated by Democritus—that man began to imitate the sounds of nature and to use them as designations. The simplicity of this theory gives it plausibility: it seems by itself to build a bridge between the cry and the designation. The sounds ceased to be mere exclamations; they were loaded with information, they contained a message.

If the first real words arose in that way, it is equally reasonable to suspect that the supply of words increased with painful slowness at first. As we know, even a human child masters only a few expressions in the six months after it has learned its first meaningful words; then there is a sudden thaw, when the child is seized with a hunger for names, and everything thereafter goes amazingly fast. Maybe the early attempts within the hunting group followed a similar course—just a few words at first, then suddenly a greatly increased need to create words and names for the shifting phenomena of the group's environment.

How the primitive man apprehended this process we can only vaguely suspect. Because we weave all our speculations out of words, we are brought up short when we try to capture a wordless image-world in our linguistic net. The being who stood at the threshold of becoming man lived in a wordless nearness to nature; the first words were born of a dim world of impressions and sensations that could not be grasped with words.

What surrounded and filled the words, at the dawn of their creation, surely must be sought in primitive man's immersion in the oneness of nature. When he began to give names to the various phenomena of nature, thing and name became one indivisible whole. To name the name was to capture the thing. In the word there was something of appeal, invocation, and compulsion. Words became part of a magic. Its innermost essence was the deep sense of the indissoluble oneness of all things. The world was not deaf and dumb; it could be understood and conjured with. In the new-minted words lay a mysterious power. In time, words were invented that were so fraught with fateful content that they were not to be mentioned; by uttering the word one could call forth what the word designated, or anger the power that lay behind and in the word. In early philosophies, the word itself became the principle of creation.

How deep-seated such ideas about the magic power of words became can be discerned, albeit dimly, in man's oldest known myths. In them, gods shaped in man's image give him the gift of language. Even as late as the time when words had begun to be fixed in characters, the mysterious power was still there: it was Odin, according to Old Norse myth, who gave mankind the runes. Prometheus, who stormed heaven on mankind's behalf, not only stole fire from the hearth of the gods for mankind, but also gave men letters, "a means of remembering all things, the Muses' mother, skilled in craft." In letters, as in the pictures that the Cro-Magnon hunter affixed to the walls of his cave, lay a trace of conjuring and ritual. It was through abstract thinking that words first came to be objectified and divorced from their absolute identification with things.

Maybe one can find in the construction of language, in the sentence forms themselves, a hidden memory from an image-world in which nature had a soul and could understand and act. In every sentence, even now, there is a subject that is assumed to be doing something even where nothing can be done, and a predicate expressing an activity that is almost always merely apparent. In every sentence one can detect an identification with human activity that seems, strikingly, to reflect the primitive man's tendency to project his own reactions and ways of doing things upon everything in his surroundings. Language allows every thing and every occurrence to act as if it were a living being: the thorn scratches me, the fire warms me, thirst afflicts me but water slakes my thirst, nature appeals to me—in effect, speaks to me. Even when we express the airiest abstractions we must fall back on linguistic constructions that seem to reflect animatistic ideas.

Here, too, one can glimpse in the child reflections from the springtime of words. His dawning consciousness is in easy communication with his surroundings. From vague perceptions and impressions he moves gradually to the stage in which he begins to catch the names of things and in which his widening comprehension of the outside world collects itself around these names as dependable landmarks and signposts. Words enable a new world to rise over the horizon that the child is eager to discover and conquer. In his earliest groping for realities, he doesn't see things as lifeless objects. They live, have motives, can act: The chair hit me, naughty chair!

The adult can never retrieve the vague, searching, fresh process that brings the child into the world of language. The adult is no longer a discoverer but a spectator. On the other hand, though he cannot relive the process, neither can he wholly free himself from it. Suddenly, a deep hole can be knocked through the layer of consciousness and fragments from the past brought to light. In a fit of anger, a man can begin to curse and kick a lifeless object as if it had purposely done him harm. Atavistic ideas of word magic can sometimes thoughtlessly slip out: If you hadn't said that, it would never have happened! Speak of the devil, he appears.

Language's fundamental tendency to express all events in human terms can be understood as a hint of a remote and common past. One may find similar hints in the dimension in which language moves. What the primate acquired in the treetops and brought down with him to the ground was a very concrete sense of space. It is striking to what a great extent the words in all languages move in geometric space. This applies even to purely abstract relations: He looked *deeper* than most . . . the motive *behind* his actions *lies* open to the light . . . but the *greatest* of all is love! Even time is apprehended spatially, as "before" and "after."

You grasp a meaning, you get a grip on a problem—it is as if your brain carried out the same movement as the ape hand when it closed around a branch in the wood of the past.

There was heat and power in the fire that Prometheus gave mankind. There was also heat and power within words. Not since the human race took fire into its service was any conquest more revolutionizing than man's acquisition of speech.

The new conquest gave mankind a double inheritance to administer. Language became a complement to the genes. What nature's great record, the genes, are on the biological plane language became on the social. Words opened up the possibility of man's overviewing and synthesizing the relations of things outside himself. Words became the cells of thought.

Speech made it possible to transmit the race's experiences from generation to generation. Over thousands of years, when the revolutionary events were few and the contacts between groups were limited, oral tradition could transmit tales of notable occurrences, observations, and thoughts through a long series of generations. It gave the tribe something to gather around, gave it history and individuality, knotted its members together. In many of the oldest tales one seems to detect elements that must have roots very far back in mankind's history.

Language's power to grow increased, and the possibilities for information to wander further through the millenia multiplied, when written language was born out of the earlier pictorial representations. The relations between sound and sign became a language's second birth. This made it possible to transmit in some thirty or forty characters, arranged in different sequences, all the knowledge that mankind has garnered, and to express all the thoughts that mankind has thought.

Language widened the space around man. The primitive man, with his intense dimensional sense, lives not only in his surroundings but with them, and he has an extraordinary feeling for their details and changes. But his grasp of space is limited mostly to the physical surroundings to which his own experiences tie him. Language opened horizons beyond personal experience. On its wings man could be carried toward new worlds, eventually to thrust into the microcosmos of atoms and the macrocosmos of galaxies.

Language also widened man's living space in time. A wordless existence has to be an extended present, in which certainly night follows day and season follows season, but in which memories from the past float around like driftwood on an ocean. Although remembered experiences can often be used to anticipate future happenings and to plan impending actions, the future lacks shape.

Language made it possible for man to see himself as a link in a chain between generations gone before and generations still to come. It gave perspective backward and a basis for planning forward. It gave man a chance to count his own annual rings and to foresee the number of his own days.

If the inevitability of his own death had earlier taken the shape of an intuitive presentiment or an obscure certainty, now it was brought home to him with aching clarity. Bit by bit, the new sense of time gave him a deeper perspective over his own existence, enabling his thought to thrust back through billions of years to visualize life's frothy rising-up and to foresee, after cosmic ages, life's ebbing-out.

The double inheritance placed man at a new border station between two worlds. Biologically, he continues to be subject to the same laws that apply to all other organisms, but with language he has, simultaneously, created a new symbol-world around himself. The thinking man is not content merely to absorb the impressions his senses transmit. He no longer meets nature openly and directly. In the structures of language, in myths, in philosophies, and in art he interprets and reinterprets what surrounds him. He observes and thinks in symbols; they have become his go-between with physical reality.

Symbols transformed the existence of the upright animal, giving it a dimension that other forms of life cannot experience.

Instead of the formless, form; instead of episodic experiences, systems; instead of instinctive perceptions, knowledge; instead of immediacy and closeness, thought's dizzying voyages of discovery through space and time!

Something you won in the process, but something lost as well.

Mighty are the domains that man, in pursuit of knowledge, has conquered, in unbroken crescendo, with sounds and signs as his armament.

But the world of symbols also has its many boundaries.

Some languages are spoken by hundreds of millions of people, others by barely a few thousands; just the multiplicity of languages builds walls between different parts of humanity. If there was an embryonic language with a common stem before man began to wander away from the central African highlands, it must quickly have branched out as the hunting bands spread out over the globe. Words, devised to ease communication within the little and burgeoning human community, have divided the great human community. The divisions go deeper than the obvious differences in vocabulary and grammar. Each language has its own atmosphere within which the words move and is an expression of a cultural pattern whose special nuances resist penetration and comprehension by outsiders.

The content of words changes, not only between different language-areas but also over time. This applies most of all to the abstractions toward which languages unceasingly move. Even abstractions were formed originally as analogies to human circumstances. Gradually, as man's circumstances and ideas change, the overtones and connotations of words also change. Thus in the meanings we give words today we fail to catch the moods these words once stirred and the ideas they stimulated in another situation, as elements of a different pattern of culture and thought.

But words also contain other obstacles, even harder to overcome.

A wanderer in the autumn meadow can catch himself thinking: It is the same with words as it is with the leaves of the trees. In their budding-time they are filled with downy freshness and explosive power. As they unfold, the forms become both more fixed and more varied; every species develops its variants—different shapes, lobes, and networks of veins—yet something in the basic plan remains common to all. Fully developed, the foliage hides in its richness some of the tree's architecture. And life is weakened in its profusion, the power runs down, everything dulls more and more until the leaves begin to wither on the tree of language.

Like the tree's leaf-envelope, language is more activity than achievement, a continuous happening, a process rather than a static condition. For words, too, growing means loss. The freshness of words' springtime is lost through satiation and fatigue—just as the adult cannot reexperience the nascent tongue's joy, in the child, when his mouth first shapes a softly humming M, a round puckering O, and a chirping R.

What we have gained for systematic thought, we have lost in immediate experience of life. Speech has enlarged our potential for orientation and overview, but it has at the same time made man a prisoner in his own symbol-world.

Our whole civilization has been swept along in a torrent of words, a torrent in which words once charged with meaning have been worn down to glosses and locutions. Words drum against our ears and are driven into our eyes. We fill our mouths with words. We use ready-made rejoinders as if we were characters on a stage. Even in our most intimate personal relationships we are often unable to let anything but stereotypes past the barriers of our teeth.

To keep silent together—how much nearness and contact it can give! Silence—how productive it can be! It is in the silences between words that the finest experiences lie hidden. The fewer the words, the greater the visions.

Yet it is as if we feared silence, or thought it unseemly.

When we try to fix in words silence's finest thoughts and visions, the inadequacy of words becomes manifest. The lucent and fragile aspect of an experience—precisely the part that we want to hold fast—is reduced to dust under the onslaught of words' blunt instruments. Even in our everyday existence, when we try to communicate to someone what we think or feel of sorrow and happiness, words often fail us. Should we wish to capture more complex events or communicate more subtle experiences, words refuse to do our bidding.

Everything is simpler than one can imagine and at the same time more complicated than one can grasp—so the *Geheimrat* of Weimar compressed his life's experience, in one of his conversations with young Eckermann. But can that true simplicity, which must be the goal of searching thought, be reached in any other way than through the comprehension of a many-sided multiplicity?

A musical score is a complicated series of note-signs, but the collective musical effect of different notes and instruments gives a unified experience. With language it is otherwise. Because of its anthropomorphic sentence construction and the watering down of words, language is already a clouded mirror for our intellect's most fragile constructions, the nuances of our feelings, and our visions' fleeting gleams. By its very nature, language follows a simple line. It is not even a chord, much less an orchestra in which lucent violins, soft French horns, and muffled kettledrums collaborate. It is a simple tune on a single instrument.

We can dream of a language that would have the musical score's ability to unify and synthesize simultaneous processes and thereby give a more sonorous expression to our deeper insights and experiences. We can dream of a wordless language, an unleafed language. In despair at our being unable to bring words and inner experiences into harmony with each other, we can try, like Faust, to break the cycle of words so as to make direct contact with life and its secrets. But no matter how we shake the bars—the symbols that the race of man once created out of the jungle's cries—we are incapable of breaking out.

Words prove inadequate for our advancing thought, which, like the tree's branches, gropes out toward the cosmos. At the same time, words block impressions that have their roots in a long-dead past.

Autumn around you. Your old companion. The bitter odors, the harsh clarity, the chill breaths through the stillness—everything glides into you, falls deeply through the layer of consciousness, and unites with sunken, seemingly bottomless memories.

Nature speaks wordlessly with you, but it does so from the other side of the bars. Beside these wordless experiences, words keep watch and importune you to formulate your impressions. Through their bars you see nature. You may stroll down the paths, letting your eyes widen with wonder and welcoming whatever you see around you, letting impressions suffuse your biological being—yet, without your being quite conscious of it, without any exact formulations finding their way out of the cerebral cortex, words are there as a shadow, the shadow of the bars.

Perhaps this has something to do with a lost rhythm. Everything in a landscape, plants and animals, is tied together by a rhythm that is felt intuitively. The primitive man, in nature, walks in that rhythm. It influences his movements and his perceptions. The civilized man no longer glides into and through the natural context. On the way from the tree to the present, the intimate and speaking contact with nature's creative powers has got broken off or, at best, been loosened. When the twigs crunch under a man's foot, it is as if a warning shout rang through the woods: An enemy intrudes! Even when you most vividly seem to experience coming closer to the source, you still remain something of an interloper in your own wood.

This you must accept. It was the price you had to pay for becoming man. The price was high, but the gain was great. To wish yourself back in a state of nature is escapism. Man's conquests cannot be unmade. From that borderland which he has reached, it is his adventure to press on further, always curiously trying, insatiably probing, his gaze searching toward new horizons.

On the other hand, what we need is an involvement in context and continuity. For lack of lines to the rear, our continued march onward could become needlessly chancy and hazardous.

LOOKING, WITH CALM IN OUR HEARTS,
AT ALL THAT SURROUNDS US

4

By mere chance were we born, and afterwards we shall be as though we had never been, for the breath in our nostrils is but a wisp of smoke; our reason is a mere spark kept alive by the beating of our hearts, and when that goes out, our body will turn to ashes and the breath of our life disperse like empty air.
From "The Vain Reasonings of the Wicked," in *The Wisdom of Solomon*

YOU, THERE! wandering among the bare trees—who are you?

Your identification card is in order, with social security number and name and a good photographic likeness and a statement of your principal occupation. You are duly entered in a book and stored in a computer memory. Every care is being taken to prevent your being confused with any of your fellow passengers in existence.

Still, who are you?

Sometimes you can be seized with the feeling that your own existence is unreal. You are walking the usual route to or from work, walking down the street with its many familiar signs and its many unfamiliar faces. Or you are on a beach, following the wave-edge where it spreads out and draws back its delicate lacework of foam, licks the lime from washed-up shells already in a gliding transition between being and nonbeing, and rubs out a pair of human footprints in the sand—everything so pressingly quiet and unreasonably clear. Or you are strolling alone in the woods, along paths you know well from many walks, but where each walk is an encounter with something different. Suddenly, the sensation of looking at yourself from outside, impersonally, can overcome you. Who is that figure on the street, on the beach, among the trees? What's he got to do with me? If he is I, what is this "I"? Out of what timbers has it been built?

Old questions, constantly repeated: Where does the individual begin? Where does he end? Philosophers' and religious teachers' answers have shifted with time and with their interpreters. Every discovery made by man's avidly searching mind has given these questions new dimensions.

When Darwin tore the veils from the past, he confirmed what a few had earlier suspected: that beyond the oneness of mankind, there is a oneness of all life. In this perspective, seeking identity becomes seeking the oneness beyond the apparent, divisive multipleness and entering into the mutual relation and solidarity of all things.

To begin with, identity is the product of powers that have worked vertically through time. But in the long evolutionary perspective all individual features disappear quickly. They drown in the anonymous mass out of which history has fished up only a few men in order to turn them over, with name and profile, to posterity—profiles that history has surely made quite unlike reality.

It is a huge collective inheritance that each parent generation molds into every new individual. The instruments that evolution plays upon are various collectives: populations, species. It is they that are dynamically workable and cohesive. Individuals are means that evolution uses and quickly uses up. Not in the separate, soon-blown leaf but in the wood as manifold unity do you find evolution's creative power. Likewise with a race's germ plasm: while individuals are born and pass away, the germ plasm streams further through the race in continually new combinations.

But dispersal of the genetic legacy does not occur uniformly. The hunting bands that once spread out from their ancient origin in Africa all over the globe carried in their genetic equipment, we may suppose, rather similar germ plasm. But the geographic dispersion followed a splitting up of the germ plasm. Certain portions of the plasm "clumped together" in smaller groups within the species: in races, tribes, clans. Man's wanderings are a tapestry whose pattern is hard to make out and has had large areas effaced, a tapestry in which nameless groups pop up, cross each others' paths, merge into one another. Within every such group, portions of the germ plasm have been compressed into streams that have crisscrossed countless times; every individual in such a group is related to himself many times over, after the most complex patterns.

You might almost wish to stay awhile with some of these earlier groups, from which you yourself have come, as well as the linguistic and cultural circle to which you most closely belong. Wish that you were able to look up your blood relations by a campfire of long ago, maybe somewhere in the Iranian highlands (which seem to have been a cradle of various Indo-European tribes, and toward which some basic similarities of language seem to point). To follow your kin, later, on wanderings toward unknown goals, the hunting packs splitting up and merging into one another but the group remaining a living organism, continually on the move and continually in transformation. To accompany them as they followed the melting ice up toward the tundra in a new land where you yourself, ten thousand years later, would stroll in the woods. To follow those other bands, too, that intruded later, after the land had become forested. To experience the confrontation between the original immigrants and the new ones, a confrontation in which blood was both shed and mixed. To try to plumb what they felt, these little bands of immigrants, as they sat gazing toward the sea-horizon, in the hushed evenings, with the unknown land behind them, the land they would take in possession. To listen to voices, silenced long ago, speaking in a language you wouldn't understand anyway.

But you would wish in vain. The doors are locked, the keys misplaced. You get no further than the fragments that can be glimpsed through the keyholes of archaeology and linguistics.

Race-, tribe-, and group-patterns are ultimately nothing but variants, in the same way that finches and roses have their variants. What is most important for you as a man is sharing in the species' common pool of genes. If the genes of all mankind could be collected, together they would be the size of a raindrop. In that drop would be encompassed the entire human heritage—all that binds us together as a species.

Your sharing in the genetic pool makes you, in a way, a part of everything that happens in the world of humankind, a part of all that has happened since man became man. In some way you were there always, in everything that happened during mankind's pilgrimage. All the aggressiveness and all the gentleness, all the pain and all the pleasure that came to man on his wanderings—you partook of it all. You were hangman and victim, master and slave; you toiled until you bled on the pyramids and you let the whip whistle over bent backs. You were the daring one with the promethean spark who defied the almighty powers, and the wretched one who cowered in fear of those same powers. All this you were, because evolution made you man.

Everything seems to have come out of Africa's human homeland. Direct lineal descent is really a descent from the primate, with human potential in him, who climbed down from the tree. All paths lead there.

Development from the primate in the trees to the individual in the present can be visualized as two cones placed base-to-base, one pointing up and the other down. The little group of primates who could first be regarded as human beings formed the point of the upturned cone. From this point, the original supply of genes were spread, in continual recombinations, on toward an ever broadening base, as man wandered out over the globe, multiplying and replenishing the earth. From a broad base, on the other hand, various hereditary qualities were gathered and molded together into the tip of the downturned cone, where the individual presently finds himself. Threads from the first human groups, spread out in all directions within the swelling human community, are again woven together within the separate individual.

On life's long journey, the tree was man's last important station. But only a station. It is generally accepted nowadays that it was about thirty million years ago that a distant ancestor branched into different lines, one leading to the higher apes and one leading to primitive men. The time that has passed since then represents only a hundredth part of life's history on Terra. Life—as we earthlings usually construe the word—is thought to have been waked on the planet some three billion years ago. Life's road is edged with wonder—if by wonder is meant events in which we may explain fairly well how something happens but stand struck with amazement that it does happen.

Life is restlessness and movement. On a sterile planet, it must have come out of a condition in which stability was lacking, perhaps arising as an inevitable result of that condition. Life was born of chemical processes, perhaps in a place where sea and land and atmospheric vapors met; there, ultraviolet solar radiation and violent electric disturbances broke inorganic matter down into a broth whose constituents, in the course of time, were rearranged (a rearrangement that man can now recreate in the laboratory). Life's first expression may have been a vague trace of irritability in the material, a dawning tendency to react to its surroundings.

In restlessness and movement life has continued ever since. It is not something that can be "placed" in a given moment, but a coherent stream that flows through the ages; it is not a condition, but a process. Basically, life is a system of chemical processes that evolution has made ever more complex but that still strictly follow the original ground rules.

Life is also structure. The amino acids and nucleic acids that were produced by the sun's and lightning's bombardment of sea and vapor linked themselves together, organizing themselves into patterns, most notably those in which carbon atoms formed the backbone.

There was probably no distinct moment of birth. One can imagine an ongoing event in which the first organic combinations were something utterly diffuse, a nutrient solution that formed a primordial oceanic soup. One can guess that a multitude of substances with different chemical properties were formed, while evolution blindly tested various possibilities. Research believes that prussic acid and hydrosulfuric acid, now deadly poisons, were among the catalysts of the first life processes.

A decisive step was taken, surely, when a few organisms rejected the ultraviolet light and began to derive energy from what we experience as visible sunlight. With its help, the water molecules were split into hydrogen and oxygen. The result was what some researchers speak of mischievously as the first great catastrophe in the history of life. The liberated oxygen was collected in the atmosphere, displacing the mixture of methane, ammonia, and water vapor that had filled it till then, and building up a blanket that shut the ultraviolet rays out. Oxygen became an "air pollution" that wiped out all organisms except the oxygen producers. Perhaps these were the ones that had acquired the strongest and most flexible structure and thus carried the future within them. Without them no oxygen-consuming organisms could have arisen—no animals, no man. An "air pollution" of billions of years ago made man possible.

Amino acids and nucleic acids remain the building blocks of all life, just as they were in the primordial sea. The combinations can change, but the fundamental structure cannot be disturbed. The route life chose upon the planet Terra, it has been obliged to continue.

Life as movement and structure can be looked at as a way in which nature organizes itself. No chemical elements are found in organisms that differ from those found in inorganic matter. Hydrogen, nitrogen, and oxygen, carbon, phosphorus, and sulfur are essential constituents in living, just as in nonliving, nature. It is in the coupling of constituent parts, in their coordination and integration, that life's distinguishing characteristic seems to lie.

In the dawn of creation there cannot have been any clear boundary between organic and inorganic nature. Nor, basically, is there any such boundary now. Our distinctions between life and nonlife, though of much practical use, are ultimately only relative. The living and the nonliving differ not in their essential character but in their relative complexity. This is a simple enough fact, but one that has important metaphysical consequences.

At some stage in nature's experimental beginning, an enclosing layer was formed around a lump of life-mass, separating an inner environment from the outer. The liquid in the bit of protoplasm inside the layer remained the same as that outside in the primordial sea. This, too, is a simple fact, and yet one that has to be kept in mind. The same salts still flow through our blood as were in the primordial sea, and they are in the same proportions. The waters that streamed through archaic seas have followed us up on land, through forests and deserts, over chains of mountains and, lately, outward in our groping attempts to reach beyond the planet. Hustling and bustling in our anthills of steel and concrete, we are really nothing but a bit of the original natural environment tied up in a bag of skin.

Perhaps manifold life as we know it began with a single cell, just as every individual living thing—tree, bird, mushroom, man—begins its existence.

The great miracle of human life is the fertilized egg cell. Though hardly perceptible to the naked eye, it contains the whole of human fate. Within it is summed up everything that has happened since the beginning of life. There the future is also foreordained. There are found detailed instructions for all the thousand billion cells into which the single cell will multiply itself.

Some cells are to work as if possessed to create a brain; yet others, a heart or a tongue, intestines or bones. It is as if all the thousand billion blindly knew their assignments and their positions, each rushing past the others to its station. Some find their way, with unerring assurance, to a molar's enamel, others find their correct position among a thousand hair follicles, still others are building different layers of skin.

A single cell cannot see or know anything of distances and shapes, colors and lights, but some millions of cells are to form a retina through which creation can look at itself. A single cell cannot hear, but some millions of them are to be assembled into auditory nerves that will capture the sighing of the wind in the treetops and the words born upon the tongues of other beings. A single cell knows nothing of its past, but millions of them are to be joined in the intricate assignment of building a hidden memory in the crannies of the back brain.

Out of the fertilized egg cell streams a mighty creative power. All cells are built of the same basic materials—the planet's commonest ones, found in rocks and seas—but each and every cell has its own special function in the organized wholeness of the human body. Yet, at the same time, each cell has its own life—is an independent creature that takes care of itself, drawing in nourishment and expelling wastes, doing its work, reproducing itself. Separately it was born, separately it shall die.

A man is a walking collection of a thousand billion independent cell lives. The sequel to the miracle of the fertilized egg cell is the ability of all these separate lives to cooperate and be integrated with each other so as to mutually build up a higher dignity of life.

The miracle of miracles is how all living things seem to have issued from a single primordial cell. How fascinating it is to imagine that life's mighty and shifting panorama developed on the same pattern as the separate life-forms!— that the fate of individuals is a fragment mirroring something of life as wholeness!

We see the primordial cell divide itself, see the cells assembled into ever more complex organisms that specialize in various directions, see dichotomous sexual organs appear that make it possible to mix the genetic material in endless variations.

We see the primordial irritability seek a lodging in simple nerve cords. In the flatworm, with two ganglia as a primitive sketch for a brain, reactions to surroundings are already joined with a certain capacity to learn. We watch the nervous system continually complexify until an intellect is almost imperceptibly released from the nerve cells' electric pulsations.

We watch a string of jelly running through a lancelet-fish harden and become a backbone still made up of the sea's primordial substances that will hold the mammal up, making it possible for the giraffe to stretch his neck and for the tiger to spring, making a group of primates into tree climbers and giving man his upright posture.

We see self-activating specks assemble themselves into a light sensitivity in cells that will eventually become an eye.

Everything has been delivered out of the latent potentialities in a planet that was sterile at first. From the single cell life starts out over the earth. From the sea it steps upon the continents and lifts toward the skies. Unceasingly it tries out new forms of expression, some of them bizarre, like those of the age of reptiles. Evolution sifts and culls the life forms. Just as the leaves of a tree wither and are shed, species also face their nights of killing frost. Some of them leave fossil remains behind; most unite with the dust of the earth, the waters, or the gases of the air.

Behind the seemingly chaotic squandering of life's various potentialities, one suspects a meaningful pattern. Through natural selection, all living things are adapted to an established environment. But the ecological possibilities that a plant or animal makes use of are ever changeable; such is the nature of life. Whenever a species is no longer able to parry the changes in its environment, its time is up.

One can guess that, on several occasions during evolution's course, the line that bore life forward to man came close to extinction. It got out of the tight places by trying new ecological possibilities. Thus man has come to be one of the outermost twigs on the tree of life.

The great adventure of our time—the greatest since Darwin—has been the voyage of discovery into the inside of the living cell and the charting of the molecules that are believed to direct the life process itself, molecules to which science has given the tongue-twisting name deoxyribonucleic acid, but that we commonly refer to as DNA.

In DNA there are few elements but infinite possibilities of variation. The acid's double helix of sugar and phosphate forms a spiral staircase in which pairs of nitrogenous bases form the treads. The bases pair off with each other according to a rigid pattern: adenine with thymine, guanine with cytosine. Out of this pattern emerge two mirror-image chains corresponding one to the other as negative to positive. Though DNA enters into an interplay of processes within the cell whose coordinating mechanism is not yet clear, nevertheless we fancy that we can see how the answer to the riddle of life lies in a harmony of simple beauty.

When a single cell can contain some ten thousand of the four bases, and the base-pairs can be combined with each other like the letters in an alphabet, the possibilities of combination become unlimited. In the DNA of the fertilized egg cell lies the separate individual's entire plan of organization. From the DNA of the primordial cell have come the orders that permitted all the species to arise. The message has become more varied and complicated as its path has grown longer. But some of the original message remains, imperishable, and calls down through the ages, calls to us from the primeval seas and jungles.

The tree whose branches sway in the winds of autumn, the wintering bird in its crown, the man at its foot—they are all of the same stuff, and within them resound variations on a theme first stated in the primordial cell.

All things form a unity: the web of many delicate relationships, in which none can live an isolated life, in which no organism can exist unconnected with the environment that is an integral part of its structure.

Under withering leaves, under the wanderer's foot: a manifold life that his eye cannot discover and his ear cannot hear. From every speck of this soil, millions of fungi send out the heavy odors that are autumn's. In every square yard live hundreds of worms, spiders, and mites, and many pounds of algae and bacteria. The earth underfoot is teeming life, and all things in that miniature world are interconnected.

The leaves have fallen and the light reaches more easily down to the soil, enlivening a multitude of microorganisms whose struggle for existence has much to do with fallen leaves. Each and every organism is specialized for its assignment. Yeast fungi take charge of the leftover sugar, which the leaves had not delivered to the twigs, branches, and trunk before being shed, and ferment it into alcohol;

bacteria drink the alcohol and give off acetic acid, which still other organisms throw themselves upon—and so it goes until leaves that once fluttered in the wind are broken down into simple salts that can be sucked up by the roots of the tree and so enter into the chlorophyll-green blood of new fluttering leaves.

What happens in the miniature world at the foot of the tree happens in creation as a whole. Everywhere connections and bonds between different organizations of living matter and, ultimately, between life and nonlife. Everywhere dependence, influence, stimulation. Everywhere everything interacting with everything.

Everywhere decay and re-creation—which need each other. Everywhere the new combinations that living evolution produces out of old elements. Individuals die and are broken down into cells and cell parts, which enter into the humus of the soil, into water and into air. But the constituents reenter new living things. Matter continually changes its address. Life eats itself unceasingly through soil and water and air that have nourished and refreshed innumerable living things since the beginning of time and will nourish and refresh new living things for as long living conditions exist on the planet. Through everything living flows a stream of matter and energy that has made guest appearances in all the shifting forms of life that evolution has produced over the ages.

Look at yourself! Into your skeleton have melted the rocks of bygone ages. Your bloodstream is moved with the tidewater's movements from a distant sea. Your flesh is composed of elements that have passed through uncountable life forms: plants, animals, other human beings. When your hand touches mine, it is the earth that grasps me.

The air washing your lungs and oxygenating your blood is filled with atoms that have visited other beings. Out of the exhalations of trees and plants you secure the oxygen without which no animal could live. With every breath you capture ten million times more nitrogen atoms than there are human beings in existence, and several million more argon atoms.

The winds have constantly intermixed them. Some come from your millions of fellow passengers in the present, some from Golgotha, some from the primate back there in the tree. Atoms from heartfelt sighs and death rattles, from sobs and laughter, from the roaring of guts and the bellowing of throats for thousands of years past—all are there. All the words ever uttered are there, stripped of meaning, robbed of sound, surviving only in the form of the air that once was forced over human teeth in jubilation and fear, in wonder and prayer, in commandments and whisperings.

The lines of connection extend not only backward but to the sides. The vertical unity that binds everything together in time corresponds to a horizontal unity in the present.

The body in its sack of skin is immersed in the external environment. The individual lives in constant physical interchange with his surroundings. The organism is the nexus of a constant going and coming of its various constituents.

The speed of this interchange varies. Biologists distinguish between different cells in the human body. Labile cells are exchanged quickly, in the course of a week to a month; they are in the outer skin, the small intestine's outer layer, the blood, and the marrow. Stabile cells, whose replacement is a matter of years or decades, these are in the bone tissues, the liver, and the kidneys. Permanent cells, finally, in the heart's musculature and in the central nervous system, where no whole cells are replaced during the individual's lifetime. In both the stabile and permanent cells, however, an exchange of molecules takes place.

Your flesh is not the same flesh that ran down childhood's barefoot paths, nor yet the same that, if you get to live some years longer, will be placed in a coffin. Daily you die a little, daily you are reborn a little.

Thus the "I"-experience, your identity, is tied in a purely physical way to a body that has garnered molecules from different times and places, from inorganic matter and from living things at all levels and in all epochs, elements that the body organizes, expels from itself, and renews through constant give-and-take with its surroundings.

And your soul?

Saying "I," one refers, usually, not to the corporeal shell so much as to the spiritual processes inside it.

Western thinkers and theologians have cherished a dualistic view of the world, in which man is torn between opposites: Caliban and Ariel, the Platonic sense-world and idea-world, the Christian temporal and eternal (a perishing body and an imperishable soul), the Kantian sensible world as against the intelligible world.

One wonders whether much of Western man's trouble through the centuries may not have proceeded from this stubbornly fixed dualism. Yes or no, it was a perfectly natural attitude—in an earlier picture of the world.

One of evolution's great wonders is how primordial irritability as the first sign of life was developed into a mind through which nature could examine and analyze itself. The difference between the amoeba's hardly noticeable reaction to its surroundings and man's creative intellectual activity appears to be so enormous that one can understand the hubris that led man to imagine that his soul was something unique, god-sent, deathless.

In the evolutionary perspective, however, there is little room for a dualistic world-view. One senses, instead, the solidarity of all things. Within the great scope of nature, body and soul make up a unity; the soul has been delivered from the womb of matter. Like the body, mind is also a product of the planet—"an earthly mind which fits our earthly body," as Sir Charles Sherrington, the philosopher of the central nervous system, put it. If one speaks, instead, of the vitalized part of matter, as the Abbé Teilhard de Chardin did, the spirit still remains matter—but matter in a higher dignity.

How matter is transformed into thought is not understood, and may never be. We know only that concealed within this miracle there is a complicated interplay of chemical reactions and electrical impulses.

In evolutionary perspective, what we perceive is a gradual awakening of ever higher levels of mind. Linnaeus, with his characteristic lack of prejudice, dared not decide whether plants, "earth's true colonizers," had the ability to feel, but he fancied that he found "a kind of lust" in them. Others have spoken of "an ability to exploit," an "instinct to solve the problems of existence," a "craving for reason" that seems to exist in all forms of life, in one degree or another.

The mushroom sinking its filaments into the birch tree's root in order to obtain the building material that the tree has taken from the atmosphere, the sunflower turning to follow the sun's path, the husbandman steering his reaper—don't they basically obey the same impulse to solve the problems of existence? Even the slime molds, those formless clumps of jelly that sluggishly advance over autumnal stumps and twigs (and may be lingering vestiges of early primitive life forms), even they must possess an embryonic exploitative ability.

Of course man cannot be the measure of all things. Isn't it presumptuous that we are able to see only instincts impelling the actions of most of our fellow creatures, while the actions of our own kind are directed by the intellect? Thus one fancies that instinct merely reacts with blind certainty in fixed situations, whereas intelligence can consider and respond to changing situations.

Humbling oneself ever so little, one will find it hard to draw sharp lines between instinct and intelligence, intuition and insight. The beaver who, long before man, was a skilled dam and canal builder; bees and wasps who, millions of years before man, had developed the technical ability to produce wax and paper; a grouse, a perch, a roe-deer who can recognize and make friends with a person approaching with good intentions, but will shun all others; animals who have developed an advanced artistic ability in ceremonies and in nest building—who dares to say they are directed only by blind instincts, that they have no intelligence with power to judge, to learn, and to predict, though it operates in other modes than man's? And contrariwise: do we really know to what extent our own actions, notwithstanding their supposed rationality, are determined by reflexes and genetically determined behavior?

Intuition may ultimately be a kind of soundboard, resonating to vibrations which started elsewhere. It may be a penetration, on a deeper level, into what unites the individual with everything else in the cosmos. Do we venture to say that it is reserved exclusively for man? Or even that it is especially characteristic of man?

What especially distinguishes man is that his mind, in the course of its evolution, has become conscious mind—mind conscious of itself. Man—as somebody once said—is a being who not only knows but also knows that he knows. Even if the purely anatomical difference between a human brain and an ape brain is small, the difference in thinking ability is enormous.

But it is a difference of degree, not of kind. What man produces by way of philosophies and symphonies, cathedrals and spaceships, does not differ, in terms of the underlying creative power, from the nest the thrush builds, the anthill to which the ant drags its straws, or the cocoon the silkworm spins.

And just as our physical being has taken in materials from everything that has preceded us, so there surge, deep in the brain beneath our observation's reach, currents from the long, long ago.

As psychologists penetrated ever deeper into the many layers of the unconscious they fancied they observed, far down in the bottom level, something that no longer pertains to the separate personality, but appears to be a kind of collective unconscious. How far does it extend? Is it something that ties together all life on this planet? Does it perhaps extend even farther?

Atop these layerings and beside the genetic code, man has, ever since he took the word into his service, created an entirely new form of inheritance—one more dynamic and more flexible than the biological.

Assume that man is, in principle, precisely the same as other higher animals in that the parents transmit to the offspring knowledge gathered by the species through generations—knowledge useful in the struggle for existence. Nevertheless, man's psychosocial development (especially during the last ten thousand years, with their incessantly increasing tempo) has given evolution a new direction in this corner of the universe.

From birth, and throughout all his twenty-five thousand days of life, man garners experiences that shape his way of thinking and being. A large part of this experiential material streams through the ages from generation to generation, depositing itself in the species, permeating every individual and becoming a part of his being. Humanity's great technical and intellectual visions are powers that work so strongly through the generations that they can no more be imagined out of the human heritage than the genes' pool can be.

Words, spoken and written, form a mighty river that is constantly widened and that slowly seeks new channels as the world picture changes. Slowly—because bobbing along in the river's backwash are ideas, norms, and prejudices that arose in quite different world-pictures but are seldom questioned as they follow the flowing onward from brain to brain.

In this way, every individual is drawn into the species'

confluent tradition. Just as the genetic germ plasm "clumps together" within humanity's various smaller collectivities, the traditional material also flows especially thick in every special cultural milieu, while at the same time every cultural milieu is formed precisely out of special traditions.

But the experiential "plasm" that a person garners reaches him not only from generations long past but also from his own time. Just as the individual is in constant exchange with his surroundings, as regards the cells of the body, so he is also in mental interchange with his surroundings. He is both sender and receiver. Everything he encounters along life's way—seas and woods and night's arch of stars, and the deeds, works, and words of men—sinks down into him and somewhere comes to rest. He becomes a part of the fellow wanderers he meets, leaving a bit of himself with them. Every experience, however insignificant it may be, or how deeply it may sink below the level of consciousness, leaves its mark.

Thus, even in the matter of the newly evolved brain's freshest layer, we are each part of a commonalty. When you get right down to it, we are collective beings whether we like it or not. Goethe observed in one of his conversations with Eckermann: "What is there good in us, if it is not the power and the inclination to appropriate to ourselves the resources of the outward world, and to make them subservient to our higher ends?"

To Goethe it seemed folly to imagine that anyone had produced anything by himself or had got it from another. He wanted to characterize his own life's work as that of a collective being called Goethe. He was, besides, no stranger to the idea that natural surroundings could affect men's temperaments: "He who, through his whole life, has been surrounded by lofty solemn oaks must be another person from him who has daily wandered in the shade of airy birches."

Thus your identity becomes, in the end, a function of your surroundings, of all you have felt and heard and observed. Identity is a mosaic in which you share separate pieces with others. Your life's work draws sustenance from countless individuals, wise and ignorant, seekers and obscurantists. Through this continual exchange the individual widens his identity in time and space. The closer men are to one another, very often, the greater the pieces of identity they exchange. In a lifelong friendship, these can become very great. As someone once put it: "Somewhere within ourselves we are always together. . . ."

There is always, naturally, a trace of indeterminacy in our experience of the world around us. Nothing is exactly as we conceive it. Every individual creates for himself a picture of the outer world that he takes pretty much for granted. We can never get to know another person's inner nature except through the interpretations we give to his actions, words, and gestures. Every individual really lives a double life, one in his own world-picture, one in the impressions that others have of him. The latter existence becomes, in certain ways, as real as the former, since the individual is judged and treated in accordance with it. Likewise with the workings of memory: in the pictures we recall from past experiences, the lighting is often changed and the details shifted. Nevertheless, in all these communications there is harmony and agreement beyond all words and beyond the reach of conscious observation.

From the world around us and from our fellow wanderers, we daily fetch a material out of which we spin our life's thread. In the end the soul may become the sum of our inborn possibilities and the experiences we garner from birth up to the advancing present and the process through which we arrange different impulses, impressions, and experiences into a coherent pattern.

When we ponder our place in this coherence, we

constantly look for starting points, perhaps because our way of thinking is spatially oriented. For the specifically human characteristics, we believe we find a starting point in the species' tree epoch and what followed immediately after. For the beginning of life itself—in the usual sense of this concept—it is natural to search back to the flowing moment of time when the first cell and the DNA-helix were formed. Nevertheless, all this is arbitrary—a cosmic short-sightedness proceeding from what Bertrand Russell used to ironically describe as a provincial and altogether exaggerated interest in our own planet.

From a cosmic point of view, so far as we know, life has no beginning and no end. Everything in the universe goes back to a few elementary particles, which can alternately appear either as energy or matter. Matter that travels at the speed of light is transformed into radiation; radiation can once again solidify into matter. We do not know the innermost nature of the elementary particles. We are beginners, haltingly trying to spell our way through the enormous book of the universe. Yet we think we know, for the most part, how the particles work.

When research had reached the conclusion that an atom consists of a nucleus with a positively charged proton, a neutron that holds the nucleus together, and one or more negatively charged electrons, which orbit around the nucleus as planets round a star, everything in creation seemed to assume a wonderful simplicity. The universe's immense multiplicity could be brought down to three fundamental building blocks. The hydrogen atom, seven billionths of a centimeter in diameter, the simplest of atoms and the most plentiful in the universe, contained a single electron circling around its nucleus at the same relative distance as the earth round the sun. The ninety-one other elements were distinguished from hydrogen chiefly by the differing numbers of protons in their nuclei. The incomparably greatest portion of even the heaviest material was empty space. If you could somehow eliminate the emptiness and press all of the elementary particles together, Mount Everest could be accommodated in a matchbox.

But of course every explanation reveals new riddles, and no explanation is so certain that it cannot be tossed aside by a new one. The beautiful simplicity didn't last long. One by one, new elementary particles were found by researchers, who began to talk of positrons, neutrinos, mesons. Several years ago, atomic research seemed to have counted some twenty different "elementary" particles.

These particles are not particles in the usual sense of the term. They are constructions of a theory that attempts to subject nature to mathematical laws; they are properties rather than tangible material objects. No one has ever seen an elementary particle or is ever likely to. However, the theory has been confirmed, so far, by such things as the successful generation of nuclear power. Yet the sudden profusion of particles confused and worried the researchers. Even if creation's innermost chambers lie beyond the longest reach of our instruments and possibly beyond the reach of our understanding, nevertheless one wishes to find, beyond the multiple and equivocal, something of the "preestablished harmony" that was on Liebniz' mind.

We may now be on the way to a new, unifying explanation. The beautiful simplicity that we thought we had espied, but that later capsized, had had a list all along: there is a positive charge only on the heavy particles. The charge on the light ones is negative. Why? we had asked ourselves. Didn't this disturb the symmetry of the universe?

It was out of such questions that the discoveries of new elementary particles came. This led, in turn, to a new theoretical world-picture having consequences that leave the layman feeling a bit faint. We believe that we now have evidence that every elementary particle has its mirror-image opposite. There exist not only atomic nuclei with positively charged protons, but also nuclei with negative charge, with antiprotons. There exist not only negatively charged electrons, but also positively charged ones, positrons. The universe can be turned inside-out! An antiproton and a positron can form an antiatom—antihydrogen. Antihydrogen and antioxygen can be combined into antiwater. Together with anticarbon and antinitrogen, they can give rise to antilife.

In this new picture of the universe, all the matter we are familiar with would have its opposite in antimatter. Like an enormous mirror of the universe of which we are a part, there would exist an antiuniverse with antiplanets and antigalaxies. This antiworld would function in the same way as our own, but we would never be able to make physical contact with it, for when matter and antimatter met, they would transform each other into radiation with an explosion of such magnitude that, by comparison, the biggest hydrogen bomb would be a firecracker.

The Swedish Nobel laureate Hannes Alfvén, who has taken part in developing the theory and, in various ways, drawing logical conclusions from it, thinks it likely that half the visible universe is built of antimatter. In this world-picture, the universe assumes a new and beautiful symmetry. It is a universe in which elementary particles with opposing charges correspond to each other as negative to positive, much as the nitrogenous bases do in the living cell's DNA.

The theory can also explain other phenomena, which earlier had capsized errant thoughts—among other things, the so-called red shift in the spectrum, exhibited by the most distant galaxies. Some astronomers had wanted to interpret this as a sign that the galaxies were being scattered, at tremendous speed, over the cosmic vastnesses. Their flight would have originated in the explosion, some tens of billions of years ago, of a primordial atom of inconceivable density, containing all elementary particles, the whole universe.

The layman has probably felt intuitively all along that that theory could not be right. The postulated existence of antimatter seems to give the red shift other, more reasonable explanations. Einstein's relativity formula combined with the new cosmic observations point to a universe without a beginning and without an end, both in time and in space.

In the light of the new cosmology we see stars born out of whirling dust clouds, lighting the remotest skies, dying in flaming supernovae that hurl their materials out in clouds from which new heavenly bodies shall again be molded. We see whole galaxies budding and falling like leaves on an earthly tree. The whole cosmos is seen as a continually ongoing creation in which inconceivably mighty powers are at work.

Since the entire universe seems to consist of the elements we know on earth, the conclusion seems inescapable that matter may well have been transformed into what we call life in many a dim corner of the universe. We are led to believe that life is simply part of the structure of the universe.

Groping for words, perhaps a bit confused about the real significance of all this, we may also sense that we are standing before life of another and greater power. Everything is composed, ultimately, of elementary particles that must be presumed to be indestructible. Isn't a sun whose metabolism transforms hydrogen into helium, releasing energy, as much alive as those creatures on a planet into whom this energy, as radiation, blows the breath of life? Is there anything in principle that distinguishes matter's pulsating activity in a galaxy from its activities in an amoeba, a leaf, or a human brain? Isn't everything in the universe, from microbes to galaxies, directed by the same law?

If everything in the universe is a cycle of cosmic birth and death, our own planet has been created, some billions of years ago, out of the same material that had gone into the making of other stars and the life forms on other planets during infinite ages past. If the universe's smallest components are indestructible, then the protons and electrons that compose your identity have, in the course of aeons, been radiation in space and matter in heavenly bodies moving through utterly other firmaments; and they have taken shape in life forms of which you can know nothing; and they shall continue to enter into galaxies and sunbeams and waters and mountains, and into new kinds of life in new worlds, long after this planet has crumbled in a cosmic autumn.

The stuff of which you are made has been joined with this earth ever since earth was kneaded together. It came from the cosmic vastnesses, and it shall return there.

It has never left eternity. It is only you that dies.

5

> *Pious I cannot call him who swathes his head in a toga*
> *Turns his face towards a stone and eagerly visits all altars,*
> *Or who prostrates himself on the ground and stretches his arms out*
> *Towards the image of gods and richly pours on the altars*
> *Four-legged animals' blood and then heaps promise on promise*
> *Pious is he who with calm in his heart looks at all that surrounds him*
> Lucretius, On the Nature of Things

IT IS ONLY YOU THAT DIES . . .

The individual is only a temporary stopping place for elements that have always existed and that shall exist always—an inn where life, on its restless journey between various life forms, has checked in for a quick visit.

The individual's function in the evolutionary cycle is to provide a transition from what has been to what shall be. "What is great in man," Nietzsche had his Zarathustra say, "is that he is a bridge and not a goal."

As a physical self, an individual is distinguished from

everything else in creation by the fact that the cosmic material of which he is composed has been joined in a combination that has never existed before and will not be repeated. In that sense, he is unique.

And yet, in a way, he certainly could declare: This life is only one of the many I have lived; my death will be only one of the many deaths I have died.

Death is just another aspect of the process of life.

Death is the wind parting the leaf from its attachment. From the branch to the ground, the journey is short.

A being whom evolution has raised above the purely vegetative cannot, however, avoid making the fundamental observation: Nevertheless, this life is mine alone. As mind, my "I" is something that did not exist earlier and shall not return. From the viewpoint of the stars, that a mind ceases must be a matter of indifference. For the individual, it is an event not to be compared with any other.

When man became man, he also gained the insight that the individual's wandering goes toward death. That insight has been hard to bear, more often than not. Man's relations with death comprehend so many nuances of thought and feeling that one must be wary of all generalizations. Nevertheless, it is clear that a very large number of men, not least those within the sphere of western civilization, are gripped with real anguish at the approach of death.

In many cases, obviously, it is more a fear of dying than it is of death. Even one who has tried to make himself so familiar with the ultimate event that he can look upon death with unflinching gaze—as the sixteenth-century French philosopher Montaigne did—may feel a distaste for, indeed a fear of, the pains, the helplessness, all the ugliness that is so often part of the passage itself.

However, many harbor a fear of death as such. The reasons for this are manifold and often hard to unravel.

Man can know nothing of the death experience itself.

No one can describe it. It is not even an experience, really, since one cannot experience nothingness. Death is the absence of presence—as Tom Stoppard calls it in *Rosencrantz and Guildenstern Are Dead,* "the endless time of never coming back . . . a gap you can't see, and when the wind blows through it, it makes no sound . . ." That everything should go on as before—"the smell of rain in the grass as I remember it, and the sigh of the wind in the trees, clouds' flying and the human heart's unease"—except your own heart's unease!—it is this that is so hard to get a grip on, for mind cannot imagine its own nonbeing.

Just for this reason, the ways in which men meet death are varied. A few who have been near death but have been snatched away at the last moment have told of a feeling of wonderful calm, of a great light, of piercingly beautiful music. Men who have not quite reached the outermost limit but have reconciled themselves to death often gain a clarified peace. Around old people who have accustomed themselves to the inescapable fact that every moment may be their last there is sometimes a gentle, bittersweet luster as they take their daily, caressing farewell of the things around them.

But for many the strange seems only frightening. Doctors and priests can bear witness that death can oftentimes be hard, very hard, both physically and psychically, sometimes to the point of raging and cursing. Even in the fullness of health, too, for how many does fear twist the bowels when their thoughts touch death!

Perhaps no one can really get to the bottom of the forces in the soul of man that cause this fear of death. Ultimately, it may go back to that biological law implanted in all life-forms—the urge to live! Surely this urge is the dominant theme of nature's great symphony, which has resounded through all the hosts of life for millions of years. Self-defense, flight from dangers and enemies, submission to the stronger—all serve the purpose of protecting life. The anguish in the eyes of a hunted or wounded animal reflects this thirst for life. But the life urge also follows a biological course: it weakens gradually until, at last, it is extinguished. When the animal feels that his time is up, he silently leaves the herd.

The biological life-urge is expressed in moments of threat and danger. In man's case, something more has been added, for in him the urge to live has taken a step further into a conscious *will* to live. Man is the only creature who *knows* that his days are numbered. He goes through life conscious of death. This makes his situation quite different. Few men are able simply to leave the herd silently and unobserved as they sense that their biological cycle is about to be completed.

Man's attitude toward death must necessarily be colored by his knowledge of life's brevity. Surely the attitudes we have today were pretty much formed simultaneously with the awakening of consciousness of death. Much of the anxiety about death that so many people feel must go back to obscure archaic concepts. In no other sphere has tradition deposited such deep layers.

How did primitive man experience death? The answers of the anthropologists are not entirely clear. We are dealing here with a remote and misty fantasy world, inaccessible to modern rationalistic investigation.

Even so, it seems to be generally agreed that realization of the reality of death came with the dawn of self-consciousness. Even though an animal holds a territory, needs to keep individual distance from other members of the species, or fights for status within a herd, none of these things is done out of an individual comprehension of being—and still less out of an individual grasp of nonbeing. Death is not a "problem." The animal that leaves the herd when its hour is come and its urge-to-live broken is obeying a biological summons whose meaning is felt but not comprehended.

When a slowly awakening consciousness of self discovered death, it must have been connected with something violent acting from "outside." The hunter downing his quarry was himself a force acting in a chain of causation. When someone in his group died without the cause being ascribable to any visible force, an intellect that had begun to grope for answers to the questions of existence may have imagined in fear and trembling that unseen powers were casting their spell—demons bent on harming man.

The dead man himself—one who had moved and breathed awhile ago and now lay there stiff and cold—became something mysterious. Thought began to fumble toward an image of a sequel in another existence. Freud has convincingly shown that in primitive thought such a continuation might be necessary. But dark fantasies crossed each other. The dead man was identified to some extent with the awesome power that had snatched him away. It was feared that he could come back and make the living go with him— perhaps as revenge for injustices or for violations of the group's norms. Obscure feelings of guilt began to bubble up.

Fear of death may originally have been fear of corpses. One tried to keep the dead man from coming back again by fastening him to the ground—burial customs that were already practiced by the Neanderthal and Cro-Magnon peoples. The gravestones in our churchyards are latter-day versions of stones rolled over graves to block the way from the dead to the living. Our mourning clothes go back to the masks by which earlier peoples hoped to make themselves unrecognizable to the dead. The German sociologist Werner Fuchs, who has studied this subject, finds even in the sublime imperative "rest in peace" vestigial incantation against the dead man's coming back.

Out of the primitive's fear of death rose a religious fantasy world. In part, it assumed the form of worshipping the spirits of ancestors. Spirits, in certain cultures, got a tremendous grip on the living. Also, it became the practice to send food and drink and weapons with the corpse, and whatever else it could conceivably want in the other life. This mortuary custom rose to monumental perversity in the pharaonic burial chambers, for which ten thousand human beings had to sacrifice their sweat and blood and earthly welfare so that one man should be able to lead a luxurious life on the other side. Above all, fantasy created powers that ruled over life and death, powers that had to be appeased with rites and nourished with sacrifices and shuddering supplications. Fear of death became fear of gods.

Christianity (like the other "higher" religions) took over such conceptual patterns and attitudes from earlier, primitive religious forms. At the same time, it inserted into its dualistic world-view more concrete versions of the Greek fantasy about a place of punishment in the other world, and the oriental fantasy about a demon crowned as the ruler of evil. These different ingredients Christianity developed into a terrible doctrine about Hell's eternal torments for unbelievers that, through the centuries, gained oppressive power over many minds. During certain periods and in certain religious communities, an anxiety-laden fixation on death rose to such a pitch that "living" became no more than a denial of life. The atmosphere could become so frenzied that men were nearly driven to the brink of suicide by fear of death.

Depth psychology has revealed that one's unconscious mind sinks deep roots into the ideas and customs of past generations, tens of thousands of years back in time. On such a central theme as death, the unconscious must be filled with survivals from the past, however rationally the everyday ego may seem to function. If the gates of Hell are bolted shut nowadays, the smell of brimstone seeps through invisible chinks and, deeper down, there must be imbedded shards of feelings molded in the childhood of the race, feelings from which arose the customs of outward show of mourning that we still unreflectingly observe.

Here may lie the deepest explanation of why so many people fear death—just as the child whose imagination has been excited by stories of ghosts and goblins may fear the dark.

The least fear of death seems to be found among those who are firmly convinced—sincere religious believers and, equally, atheists who have a coherent philosophy. But both groups are small. It is in the wavering light of uncertainty that ghosts flit about. A strikingly large proportion of those who call themselves Christians seem to be gnawed by fear of death. On the other hand, the secularized western man who has given up the old faith has access to hardly any "technique" for coping with distress and loneliness, and still less the problems of dying and the sorrow of the survivor, other than technique clothed in religious terms.

Much depends on the fact that death has become, in our rationalistic modern times, something anonymous and formless. The whole present-day social environment, with its dispersal of the extended family and its crowding of people into denser and denser settlements, has left no place for death in the everyday life rhythm. The progress of medicine has banished sickness and death to the impersonal milieu of the hospital.

Death is suppressed. That both the poles of life, begetting and dying, should be surrounded with so many taboos and so much artificiality is among the distortions in the shape of man's society in recent times. In the case of the sex life, the veil of prudishness has lately been pulled aside. After rebound in the opposite direction—perhaps a kind of inverted bigotry, and understandable as such—we may dare to hope for the emergence of a more natural attitude toward the act that is prerequisite to bearing the seed of life onward through the race.

Death, on the other hand, still remains almost unmentionable, unless it occurs in the mass format of accident or war, or in the titillating thriller format of movies and other fictions. Recent attempts to undramatize it have had little success. The consciouness of death is shut out of everyday life. Around a deathbed there often flourishes a hypocrisy that denies to the dying person his fundamental right to be told the truth of what lies ahead and to make what he considers good use of the time remaining to him.

Chase the devil from the front door and he'll come in the back. We can drive death out of our conscious minds, but not out of our unconscious. And there it can become a despot. Much of the pressure of our work and of our pursuit of pleasure, nowadays, is nothing more than flight from alienation, an alienation that comes from our losing touch with life's own rhythm, of which death is a part. Man has an agonizing need to get into balance with himself. Relating to death in a more natural way might help.

Already, death is there within you, working in your flesh and your guts, in your pulse and your brain. As the days of life go by, he takes you over more and more.

In the great fabric, "death" and "life" are not opposites but two threads in the same pattern. In a way, living means dying, since all individual life forms a curve, in which growth turns to decline. Indissolubly, life and death enter into a totality in which the deaths of individuals are necessary to the continuing of life.

It is with this, with nature's great rhythm, that the individual needs to go along, not reluctantly but as an obedient participant. The Swiss psychoanalyst Carl Jung speaks, in an essay, of the secret hour, at the midpoint of life, when life "turns," when death is born: "From the middle of life onward only he remains alive who is ready to die *with life.*"

A simple, unsentimental, and fearless familiarity with death can give our days a richer content. A sober consciousness of death can be the servant of life.

Our having a more matter-of-fact attitude toward death could have several consequences. Among other things, it could lead to our erasing the many prejudices we have about a death that anticipates nature's own life-ending process.

Within the sphere of western civilization, so full of Golgothas, so accomplished in war and gladiatorial games, inquisitions and hangings, burnings-at-the-stake and gas chambers, the attitude toward a person who has tried to take his own life has been judgmental and condemnatory. The suicide has not been permitted to rest in consecrated earth (consecrated earth? as if all earth were not alike!); the unsuccessful suicide has been punished—if not with the death sentence, then nearly.

If your life is your own, your death must be your own. It is, after all, the last thing the individual has at his disposal. If your body has broken down to the point that you can expect nothing more of life; if your pain is terrible or you see senility at hand; if, in some other way, you are finding life almost impossible to endure—in such situations it surely must be a basic human right to make your own decision. It is also honorable to know, like a courteous guest, when to express your thanks and take your leave.

Suicide becomes degrading when it is used to evade problems in a way that imposes burdens on other people. There is an ethical requirement, a responsibility that goes beyond the grave, not to create suffering and difficulties for others. There is an aesthetic aspect, too. In modern society, not only is it difficult to die outside the hospital without making trouble for others, but besides that so many suicides are so ugly. It is now regarded as legitimate to give public education on how to prevent the conception of new life. Maybe it would be just as legitimate to teach how to end one's life as neatly and with the least trouble to others as possible.

When a third party enters into the decision making

between the individual and death, then the problem gets more complicated. With technical appliances such as respirators and heart-stimulators, the doctor can now maintain sparks of life long after the body would otherwise have broken down by biological processes. As techniques improve, these possibilities are going to increase in number. More and more often the physician will face tough decisions: to use his technical skills and appliances to keep a fading flame of life flickering for as long as possible, or to shorten the suffering by stopping the treatment. For the easy conscience that the former choice can give the doctor, the patient may have to pay with an extended death struggle. Surely in many cases it would be more humane to shorten the suffering and let a dying man and his relatives take a calm leave, without painful and troubling technical appurtenances.

Thus far one can speak of a passive euthanasia. But the next question is, if one can break off a treatment, why wait then for death to strike? Doctors can tell you how desperately the incurably ill may crave release. Why can't the doctor grant the last wish of a dying person through active euthanasia, when the sick person is himself incapable of cutting the thread of life? How is one to distinguish in principle between euthanasia for the incurably ill and, at the beginning of life, abortion for medical reasons?

There is also an ethical requirement imposed on those who are closest to the person. Our sorrow is not simple compassion for him, as we so wish to believe. It is our own loss we bewail, ourselves we are sorry for when we mourn. If the relatives of a man dying in agony cannot admit that death will bring him a release he longs for, it probably is not the sufferer for whom the relative feels the most sorry.

These problems are loaded with emotion and are essentially difficult. And yet it should be possible to consider them openly, cleansed of the dross of prejudice. Respect for life need not mean that death is to be regarded as the great enemy, to be held at bay for as long as possible no matter what the cost. Respect for death is also needed.

Death is a part of the mystery of life, but there is nothing mysterious about death itself. This one can dispassionately perceive. The inflexibility of the life cycle can be accepted. But that is not always enough. Many feel that they are faced with a brutal absurdity. It is not the pain of withering's long decline that frightens them, nor even the moment of death. It is the thought—warded off, despite all reason—that one's own mind shall someday be extinguished, shall disperse like empty air.

Common sense tells us that grass must wither, leaves fall, stars burst, all in order that new life shall arise. One can accept the fact that this same law applies to one's fellow-men. Yes, one can even imagine one's own bodily death, seeing oneself as a shovelful of ash that somebody carries away in an urn: that need not trouble one, and it may, indeed, give one a feeling of relief. But this is something else: that mind itself, with which one experiences life's beauty, struggle, and joy; the feelings that well up out of the depths; the experiences that one has laboriously and strenuously garnered; the thoughts that one has thought—that all this shall someday not exist, shall altogether cease to exist!

Evidently many experience what the Swedish writer Herbert Tingsten referred to as a kind of continual, haunting fear that their own reality will be wiped out, will disappear. You have thrown overboard the entire supernatural, you don't believe in any afterlife (in the religious sense), and yet you find it outrageous that you, that all that has been assembled from different times and places and formed into your conscious identity, should simply be extinguished. There are agnostics and atheists who, with their intellect, embrace without reservation a materialistic picture of the world but who nevertheless characterize themselves, against reason, as death-protesters.

What is it that is so extraordinary that one will not give it up? It is one thing for mind to have a hard time picturing its own nonbeing, another thing for mind to refuse to accept nonbeing. If such protest is to have any real meaning, it should include all degrees of mind, from the amoeba's hardly noticeable irritability right through to the human brain's noble and less-than-noble thoughts. And all degrees must survive, not in any collective mind-mass, but individually—in some sort of cosmic rag-and-bone shop for second-hand minds. Naturally, one hasn't thought of it that way. If one takes, instead, a position that is impossible from the evolutionary standpoint, the position that only man (and any other equally intelligent beings elsewhere in the universe) is capable of producing anything that, from the cosmic standpoint, is worth saving, then, in the name of logic, one would have to leave out everything in our unconscious that we have carried with us from earlier forms of life. This would leave us with what has been built out of those experiences a man, in his one short life, has acquired. But these have been collected through the senses of the living body, through what the nerve endings in skin, eye, and eardrum have captured from the external world. One can hardly imagine this existing without connection to the body. Even if such were the case, even if, through the action of forces we do not understand, some part of the nonmaterial ego were to continue as some kind of quivering leftover of mind—are we really so sure this would be something to wish for? If we think it through, wouldn't such an eventuality be even more frightening than annihilation?

To pretend to a special place for man, to be unwilling to accept for our own species the same fate that is accepted as natural for other life forms, wouldn't this be a profound betrayal of the solidarity of the individual and nature?

All our experience, so far as it now extends, testifies that when the brain dies, the individual mind is extinguished.

For a time, one will be "coming back" as an unsteady and fading memory, in such a quickly attenuated form to exist awhile in the gravitational field that, stronger or weaker, surrounds a man. But sooner or later one's work, whatever one has accomplished, will be forgotten, and one's name will be rubbed out. All that was an identity will sink down into the nameless mass of the past and gone. It is easy enough to see why this prospect can sometimes cause shudders of fear. And yet doesn't the very certainty of it contain something more soothing than frightening!

For your mind to be extinguished is no different, in a way, from your not having been born at all. What's to be afraid of in that?

But who can pretend to be altogether sure of himself? Not even the person who believes himself ready to meet death calmly, who is quite confident that it is nothing much, can be certain how he will react at the time when his senses are muffled in fatigue and dark voices start their muttering in his unconscious. Could one say a prayer, just one—but to whom?—it might well be this: Let me die with dignity, with my humanity intact!

However, it seems certain that we are at the threshold of a revolution in thought, a revolution whose attitudes will gradually come to penetrate men's minds as powerfully as fear of the gods and fear of death suffused the minds of past generations. What happened when man discovered death was that he broke free of the instinctual conformity with the biological cycle that distinguishes other forms of life. His mind, during its early gropings, tried to get a grip on things through various primitive explanations of death. Seeing as mind has evolved beyond these explanations, it ought to be able, on a higher plane, to rediscover its intuitive connections with the larger context.

Once, when Albert Einstein was asked by Hedvig Born if he ever felt a fear of death, he answered: "Why should

I? I feel such solidarity with all living people that it is a matter of indifference to me where the individual begins and where he ceases!" On another occasion, he told one of his colleagues how wonderful he found life, how he enjoyed it. But, he continued, "were I to know that I should die within three hours, I should not be very impressed. I should consider how I could best use those last three hours putting my papers in order, and then I should lie down quietly."

As it turned out, Einstein had a hard death, according to his son's report. Even so, the attitude toward life that he expressed ought to be a natural result of the new horizons that research has opened up for man during recent generations.

After innumerable vain attempts to find his place in creation, man has, through knowledge of evolution, found solid ground to stand on. The natural sciences, especially the new cosmology, have pulled man down from the pedestal on which he had, in collusion with ignorance, earlier placed himself. Searching thought, born of matter, has transformed man's celestial home, with all that it contains, into a fleck of the wave froth from a cosmic surf in which billions upon billions of galaxies gleam and vanish and arise again.

In the seething vastness of life and in the myriad interrelations among all forms of life, there is no place for individual self-centeredness; there, to protest or to crave is equally irrelevant. Much in the new cosmology and biology has turned everything upside-down so quickly that we haven't yet had time to absorb it. Even a person who intellectually embraces the new picture of the world, and does so unreservedly, is often still tied to old conceptual patterns by thousands of threads invisible to himself. And yet one seems to divine, somewhere in the boundary zone between suspecting and knowing, that the revolution of thought now under way will come to free man from archaic ideas that have been the source of so much fear. One who has become accustomed to wandering in the wide new fields will be unwilling to turn back into the little furrows in which fear for his own fate thrives.

Earlier systems of thought and belief stopped at earthbound horizons. How much more powerfully should this invite our devotions: that on a little speck in the universe there is a species in which billions of years of evolution have recently led up to a mind through which the cosmos can experience itself and nature can investigate its own nature; a species through which the universal material has so realized its possibilities that it can itself try to solve life's riddles, piercing to its own innermost and listening to the crash of worlds so distant in space/time that mind knows of them only from signals that left their source billions of earth-years before this earth came to be and are only now arriving here—and, in this way, catching a glimpse, if ever so fleeting, of life's breathtaking totality!

But nothing comes easy, nothing is unequivocal. An objection lies in wait for us, and it will not fail to be heard: Man, we are told, cannot do without the support of myths. They are connected with his deepest needs. Without myth to structure his life he is incapable of bearing the weight of the cosmic vastness. Perhaps he can be liberated from the fear of death. But if the individual sees himself only as a temporary container for the seed of life, on a little speck in the universe that is itself whirling toward its own planetary death and the cosmic forgetfulness, the consequence may be that he will feel that nothing is worth living for and that it doesn't matter how he acts.

This objection may be understandable, but the conclusion drawn from it is quite untrustworthy. Religious views that refuse to take the consequences of thought's revolutions are inexorably going to be borne to the side of the stream of development, like it or not. When myths, in their concrete expressions, are no longer in tune with man's new certitudes and convictions as to truth, they will lose whatever supportive power they may once have had. It is then that emptiness will threaten. It is impossible, however, to close one's eyes to the fact that the new cosmology, superficially considered, may lead to conclusions tending to rob the individual life of deeper content and meaning.

Such conclusions would miss the essential feature of the evolutionary perspective. What gives a human life its nobility, even its solemnity, is that the temporary but unique combination of body and spirit in each life is the result of an unceasing and cumulative process over a period of billions of years on this planet—that, ultimately, each human life is something that the cosmos, in all its stunning impersonality, has worked upon and prepared through the endlessness of ages. What, superficially regarded, may seem to make individual life meaningless, can, in a deeper perspective, come to inspire man with a sense of reverence and humility.

Man has shrunk. Inconceivable space whirls round his littleness. But he need not, therefore, shudder with Pascal: "The eternal silences of endless space frighten me!" It is precisely in his littleness that man can experience the greatness in his having been part of the immensity.

Will this hold? Yes. Hold it shall and hold it must. They who grew up under other guiding stars may feel, for a fleeting moment, some sting of loss for the trust in a good Father that a fervent belief confers, a Father in whose arms they would rest one day. There is so much simple goodness and beauty in that belief. But there is no way back to it, and one does well not to wish there were. In the immensity that has opened before our observation and thought there is no place for any personal god or any personal immortality; in this certainty lies a great relief. In place of the discords and indeterminacy of the dualistic world-view, a holistic view emerges, one in which all processes—cosmic, biological, spiritual—are united. To experience that unity is to know a profound peace, at its best perhaps not far from the happiness that Spinoza dreamed of—the *hilaritas* that spreads a cool September light over existence.

"Piety," Lucretius called such an attitude toward life when, in the century before Christ, the Roman philosopher-poet contemplated the nature of things with a visionary power that still grips us.

Even so, there are questions that stubbornly persist, old questions in new trappings. Not even one who treads the new paths can shut his mind to what our human understanding apprehends as discords in the great music. Why does the stuff of which the world is made take shape in so many imperfections? How can the elementary particles, swept together from the cosmic vastnesses, possibly have combined into such grotesqueries as the cruel monster world of the reptile age, for example? Why is there so much that seems, to our understanding, so ugly? Why all the suffering—suffering that, were it collected from all the ages, ought to be powerful enough to burst stars?

It was probably the sufferings and imperfections of existence that gave rise to the dream of a kingdom of perfection on the other side that is so important a part of the dualistic world-picture. The wisdom of the east chose, in part, another way than the religious dreams of the west. When, twenty-five hundred years ago, Gautama Buddha meditated at the foot of the holy bo tree, the schemes of existence that rose up before him included no directing godhead and had no place for any immutable soul. All was mutability. Reality was impersonal and beset by accidental impulses from the inexpressible. Death was not something that "befell" man but the dissolution of mind into components that kept up a perpetual circulation. Liberation from the suffering and imperfection of existence came about not through one's deliverance into eternal life but through one's entering into nirvana, into extinguishment, into a deathless place, into a nonexistence in which nothing individual could exist.

Thus early Buddhism anticipated much of what

modern research has arrived at. In practice, however, Buddhism's striving toward nirvana gave rise to a contempt for life. Life was something you were sentenced to. The "good" was not existence but nonexistence.

One who sets his feet on the ground of a world-view based on natural science has neither heaven nor nirvana to run to. As he tries to deal with the problems of suffering and imperfection, he is obliged to accept reality as it is. To affirm science's world-view must imply that one affirms a comprehensible existence. It is through our living—here and not in any other world—that we can experience being a part of the great oneness.

But this also means that we must become accustomed to not having a permanent anchorage; our anchor will drag continually over new bottoms in the ocean of space/time. Science's world-picture is relative. What it reveals is not ultimate truth about nature but simply what we experience, with our gross minds, as reality. Neither is it a picture that rests in static stillness like the dream of a heaven or a nirvana. It is a picture that constantly shifts and is as dynamic as life itself.

The universe surely conceals many surprises for man the seeker. Science's convictions of truth today are going to be otherwise tomorrow. Like Darwin, you must always be prepared to sacrifice the explanations that you value most, if need be, as new facts come over your horizon.

And not only is the universe stranger, surely, than we can now imagine, it is almost certainly stranger than we shall ever be able to understand. Our knowledge can never be other than fragmentary. Every new discovery gives birth to new questions. To the ultimate discovery, what was the beginning of everything, we are unlikely ever to reach.

But the restlessness and impatience that man can feel about this fact—are these feelings basically anything but the remains of our arrogance, an arrogance that should have been curbed by our clearer view into the cosmos? What does the ladybug on your hand know of your thoughts? We, so recently waked to conscious mind upon an insignificant speck in the vastness, how can we expect ever to understand the power behind everything, however much (by earthly measure) we may widen the limits of our knowing?

We had better get used to our own ignorance. The greatest illusions arise out of our being ignorant of that ignorance. Besides, if we did come to know everything, wouldn't much of the excitement go out of life?

Deep insight lay in the words with which the great spiritual experimenter of Weimar summed up a rich life's experiences: The thinking man's greatest happiness, he declared, is to have succeeded in investigating what can be investigated, and calmly to honor what cannot be.

There are worlds beyond worlds beyond the worlds in the world—worlds we cannot reach because the mind's barques are too flimsy. How far the odyssey of our thoughts will carry us we cannot yet know. But we feel we must go on.

One evening, when heaven and earth bend near and the stars seem to hang like golden fruit in the branches of the trees, you can let your fancy flutter toward the deep blue.

Does some reality exist that intuition grazes against even though our senses cannot capture it? When the individual dies, the elementary particles remain, indestructible. These have shown themselves capable of creating not only waters and mountains, stars and brains, but also mind. Does a tendency toward mind exist in even the smallest particle, just as there exists a tendency to build up ever more complex molecular organisms? Man seems to find, in the brain's nethermost level, a collective unconscious; does it connect us, ultimately, with not only all the life forms on this globe but also with some structure in the universe that man might describe, for want of a better word, as spiritual? Does some kind of "power of thought" also exist in some of the heavenly bodies in the universe—for example, as the scientist Haldane believed, in the dense material at the heart of white dwarf stars? Does the same creative power that builds galaxies move within us when we think and when we sense?

What that power is, we cannot imagine. Our picture of the cosmos has dimensions too few and too simple. It has been so short a time since we climbed down from the tree. Perhaps we will gradually become capable of experiencing existence in additional dimensions. Just as we sometimes seem to catch wavering glimpses of the fields of force that, beyond the known senses, link living beings on our little globe, perhaps one day we may catch glimpses of fields of force and communications in the cosmos that today we cannot even begin to suspect.

Science can represent reality only in symbols. Similarly, the religious systems of belief were once (before their forms became rigid) time-limited attempts to capture in symbols the reality that man seemed to experience. If you strip away from their creeds all the confused dogmas, which have clarified nothing but made much unclear, the mystery that remains is the unconscious experience of oneness with a cosmic Other. Is this so very different from what those without a formal creed can experience: intuitive impressions of nearness to a "something" in nature beyond what intellect can define?

Evening. Trees. Stars. Fantasies that whirl up toward the blue.

Earth under you.

On this planet, man became the vertical animal, like the tree raising himself from the ground, groping toward the cosmos. At life's decisive moments, man again seeks the earth's horizontal: in the embrace where he molds the possibilities of the human inheritance into new life, in death when he reverts to the basic components of new life. His mind is an earthly mind, colored by the planet out of which it has been begotten. But always it must reach up toward the infinity from which the planetary substance once came.

When the path begins to slope downward you feel an increased eagerness to make use of time—to "use the time you have left."

Past and gone: all those mornings you have had, mornings you filled with expectations and intentions . . . all those days that were so very different from what you wanted them to be. Nothing complete to linger upon . . . mostly trifles . . . too little wanted, too little dared.

When the curve of life has turned, you feel a greater need to fill every moment with something, whether some task that you tell yourself you want to accomplish before you're through—however conscious you may be that soon thereafter the work will be effaced—or such essential things as following the movement of clouds, listening to the wind wandering over the meadows, or lapsing into a wordless sympathy with her, the sharer of your days and nights. Just don't let the moments run away empty! Hold fast to the feeling: this I am experiencing, and now.

Feelings to linger upon, memory pictures on pure and simple themes blending with the impressions of the present:—

Early mornings on the water, when the dawn breeze slips over the fjord. The sky, transparent, unites itself horizonless with the sea. Something in you surges with the morning swell, and all is timeless contentment.

Day in the mountains. The splendid exertion of climbing, then the relaxing. A moment to look around and ponder before you begin the climb down. Glacier crowfoot springs up at your feet. The beginning of a brook frets the edge of your hearing. The landscape's big picture. You drink sunshine, you breathe hugely.

Your wood at sunset. The living silence, in which the day's pressure on the senses loosens. The sun bends toward the horizon, making shadows of trees and bushes, shadows that slowly wander over soft moss and the undulating line of the stones. A moment when you can imagine finding the reality of life itself in the gliding changes of the forms.

Oh yes, there is of course a quiet sadness in the knowledge that you will soon be taken away from all this. But greater still is the joy, equally humble and wonder-struck, that for a moment this bit of the cosmic substance got its chance to glimmer as mind in the great drama.

SOLIDARITY WITH LIFE

6

Concern for man himself and his fate must always form the chief interest of all technical endeavors. . . . Never forget this in the midst of your diagrams and equations.
Albert Einstein

OUR SPECIES BECAME *Homo technicus*—technical man.

We have not yet lived up to the designation that—overestimating ourselves?—we preferred to give our kind: "Homo sapiens"—wise man.

Ever since the primate climbed down from the tree and straightened himself up from the ground, the dominating aspect of man's evolution has been technological development. In comparison with biological development, it has gone extraordinarily fast. Man has utilized the heritage of his tree sojourn—the hand's ability to grasp and the brain's ability to correlate—for one technological transformation after another. During the first millions of years these efforts were fumbling, but after man became an earth cultivator and a village dweller, the transformations occurred at a constantly accelerating pace, right up to the feverish tempo of our own time.

Technology breeds more technology.

Though human brains and human hands accomplish every technical advance, it is as if a self-activating power moved in technology, driving it onward in unrelieved crescendo. The technological way of life that man has developed is a product of his brain. That way of life, in its turn, affects man's ways of thinking, being, and acting.

There are many connections between the technological spiral and that of population. In this century man's reproduction has achieved such a rate that world population is doubled in thirty-five years. In the same way, the rate of technological development has been doubling in the course of each generation.

The American futurologist Alvin Toffler has tried to illustrate this steadily quickened pace of development by dividing the last fifty thousand years of man's existence into lifetimes of just over sixty years. The computation gives us eight hundred lifetimes. Of these, six hundred fifty were lived in and around caves. Only during the last seventy has it been possible to communicate from one lifetime to another through writing, and only during the last six have the masses had any contact with the printed word. To measure time with any precision has been possible only during the last four lifetimes, and only during the last two have ordinary people been able to use electricity. The overwhelming majority of the material things that we use in our daily lives have been developed during the present lifetime, the eight-hundredth.

A person who finds himself past middle age was, in a way, born in the middle of man's history. In technological terms, today's world is as distant from the world of his childhood as that was from the Stone Age.

Tragically, mankind's increased technical ability has coincided with an increasing insensitivity to nature's interplay of balances. Together, they have begotten an arrogance that has led man to think himself lord over everything else in creation. This is reflected in several of man's systems of thought and belief. Both the ancient Mosaic creed, to some extent refined and focused by Christianity, and the original Marxism, mostly coarsened by its interpreters, have expressed, each in its own way, this hubris of human thought, and both have contributed to maintaining it.

Primitive man, apprehending nature as animate and himself as a part of nature, had powerful taboos against interfering with it. If he was obliged to fell a tree, he preferred to set another in its place. The Hebrew creation myth dethroned nature, making it serve man. His was the God-given role of mastering everything else in creation, for all things, even the sun of day and the sparkling stars of night, were there for his sake. Into Marxism's materialistic view of history, similar ideas were woven: work was that process through which man subdued nature and shaped its material to suit his needs.

Thus man has increasingly used his brain and nature's other resources to detach himself from the natural world out of which he came. His technological progress has been built upon disastrous illusions.

We have only one environment. No organism can exist unconnected with the environment, which enters into its structure. Every organism—worm and bird, tree and man—is subject to environmental laws.

That part of the earth in which life (as we mean it) exists and carries on metabolism is called the biosphere, the sphere of life. It is a sphere in which the solid, the liquid, and the gaseous continuously, and according to the most intricately spun patterns, cooperate with each other, a sphere in which solar energy can act and in which water, the simplest and most notable substance in all chemical combinations, is found in sufficient quantity. The biosphere consists of the sea of air next to the earth, of an inch-thick skin of soil penetrable by the sun, and of the light-accessible layers of water in oceans, lakes, and streams.

Within this sphere, life carries on a constant barter. Sea and rock and air and life are integrated with each other and trade components with each other. The elements essential to life are in constant cycle between water and earth and atmosphere and a myriad of changing organisms. What we call life is in itself a cycle, at the same time that it is a part of the greater cycle.

In life's cycles, some of the lightest elements play the heaviest roles.

From the standpoint of life, the most remarkable element may be oxygen, since all life that exists on earth has been made possible by the great oxygen revolution of billions of years ago. Oxygen comes from life and builds up life: what plants breathe out, animal life breathes in. Life is bound up with the circulation of oxygen, as this circulation now occurs. Oxygen accounts for a fourth of all the atoms in living material, and a fifth of the sea of air, life's great reservoir, is filled with oxygen.

Together with the universe's fundamental element, hydrogen, it forms a liquid that flows through everything living—in mixtures approaching what we call water.

With the sun as the source of energy, water can be combined with carbon into organic matter. In the biosphere, various carbon compounds are in a constant ongoing dynamic process of creation, transformation, and dissolution. In the breath of life, carbon plays an opposite role to that of oxygen: the carbon dioxide that animal life breathes out, plant life breathes in. But the barter economy is more complicated than that. With the leaves that fall to the ground, carbon atoms enter into the processes of the soil, some finding their way through the roots back to the tree, others returning to the atmosphere. At the same time, with the help of winds and waves, a dynamic exchange of oxygen and carbon dioxide is going on between the oceans and the sea of air.

In another cycle, nitrogen describes its continual circulation. It is there in every breath drawn by animal and man, from life's first gasping for air to the final death rattle. The sea of air surrounding the globe is four-fifths nitrogen. The supply may seem unlimited, but actually it sets a very specific limit to the life-mass that the globe is able to maintain. Nitrogen is basic to the nourishment of the vegetative growth upon which secondary life, animal life, is destined to depend.

After the four principal elements come a pair that enter into the processes of life in slight but indispensable quantities. Sulfur gives the proteins the three-dimensional character without which they would not be able to fulfill their functions, so important to life. Phosphorus provides the indispensable and universal fuel for all biochemical processes in the cells, and no life, not even the most microscopic, is possible without it. On land, phosphorus sets limits to the quantity of life; in the oceans, iron plays the same role. Thus, there is no more life on land than the limited—very limited— supply of phosphorus can fuel, no more life in the water than the short supply of iron permits.

These elements, which life on this speck of space chose once and for all as its building blocks, enter into sensitive and complicated cycles that have been fashioned over billions of years. The atoms of life continually wander through gaseous, liquid, and solid combinations and through different forms of life. If the biosphere is to function harmoniously, these atoms must, after their guest appearance in living matter, resume their course through the cycle. It is thus they can serve the new, the coming life.

If the pace of their circulation is disturbed or the course of their circulation is altered the balance wheel of the cycle falters, with all the consequences that that entails for the processes of life. If a substance becomes too scarce in its natural environment, the foundation of life is altered. If it becomes too plentiful or is dumped into surroundings where it doesn't belong, it can act as a poison. Life's balance is extremely delicate.

It is just this balance that *Homo technicus* is disturbing radically. All the elements that, together with life, take part in the great circulation—water, air, soil—are being changed by him. Soon they will have quite another structure than that which was gradually developed out of nature's creative processes.

Water surrounds life and is part of life. A single drop can contain thousands of individual microscopic lives. Man is a walking vessel seven-eighths full of water.

Water is the earth's most plentiful substance. In the zone where the crust of the earth contacts the layers of the air, water builds a sphere in which life can develop. In its interplay with the various elements, water itself can shiftingly emerge as ice, liquid, or cloud. Like no other element, it shifts among the solid, liquid, and gaseous states and yet remains always water.

Hydrologists have calculated that the globe accommodates about three hundred sixty trillion gallons of water in various forms. Ninety-seven per cent of it surges in the oceans' brine, and most of the rest is frozen into the ice-mantles of the poles and into the glaciers of the high mountains. Only seven-tenths of one per cent of the world's water resources is found in lakes, rivers, and groundwater, and as water vapor in the atmosphere.

It is on this seven-tenths of one per cent that all life on the earth's land masses depends.

This water, too, comes mostly from the oceans. The sun uses a third of the energy it sends to Terra lifting water from the surface up into the atmosphere. A smaller part vaporizes from the soil and lakes and transpiring plants. The incomparably greatest quantity evaporates from the open reaches of the seven seas.

A tenth of the water that is lifted from the oceans drives across the land: clouds are water that streams through the atmosphere like currents through a sea. It is chiefly this water from the oceans that makes the continents green.

The greater part of the water that falls on land finds its way through the rivers and back again to the sea. A portion filters down through the sieve of the soil to the groundwater level; the soil in the forests is especially loose and permeable. But there is also a force that raises groundwater, the capillary action, which sucks up part of the deep waters.

The roots of trees can carry it further, into that process beside which all others dwindle—the process, basic to life, in which the sun, through photosynthesis, causes water and carbon dioxide to form carbohydrate. Part of the water that is sucked out of the ground finds its way through the needles of evergreens, and through the leaves' fine nets of veins, out again into the atmosphere. Trees also make the air soft and the climate agreeable for animal life.

Water vapor in the atmosphere is the reservoir of the hydrological cycle. At any given moment there is ten times as much water in the atmosphere as there is in all the rivers of the globe. Yet if the atmosphere were wrung dry, it would only suffice to yield slightly more than one and a half inches of rainfall. The reservoir must be constantly refilled if the cycle is to function.

The cycle itself goes back to the beginning of the world. The water that the sun is now lifting from the oceans and the clouds dropping on the land was part of the water vapor that oxygen and hydrogen formed when earth was a glowing ball, and it was part of the downpour that washed a still-sterile world when the ball cooled and the vapor condensed.

In the dampness that the autumnal earth sends up to meet you, there are drops from the very primordial sea in which life began, from the wine that refreshed the wedding guests at Cana, and from the cooling-water recently expelled from an atomic reactor on some distant coast. Through billions of years, the hydrological cycle has carried water molecules round the planet in eternal repetition of evaporation and run-off, precipitation and tiny tricklings through porous soil. Life, which began in the primordial sea's bag of waters, can only exist in a constantly ongoing baptism.

Everything living thirsts for water, and man is the thirstiest of all. The greater his distance from the natural condition, the greater his thirst. In contrast with nature's other gifts, water requires no work to change it; it is simply there for the using. Because of its versatile usefulness it has achieved a special place in man's economy.

By the World Health Organization's minimum standard, every inhabitant of earth ought to consume—directly or indirectly—some forty gallons of water daily, on the average. In reality, the inhabitant of a large city in an industrial country consumes as much as twenty times more than most inhabitants of "underdeveloped" countries. According to this computation, our global water usage should amount to about a hundred thirty billion gallons daily. If man's thirsting fields and factories are included in the computation, the sum will be multiplied. Even so, compared with the globe's total water resources, all of man's needs are hardly more than a drop in the bucket. However, man depends most on just a fraction of one per cent of the grand total—that is, on the relatively small amount of fresh water. Hence, the pressure on resources is becoming severe.

Much too much so. In many places, groundwater reservoirs that were filled during many thousands of years have already been emptied or forced down, sometimes to depths of many hundreds of feet. As a result, the ground has hardened and is no longer saturated by the rain. This, in turn, can lead to the rainwater's running back to the seas more quickly than it can be replenished by the clouds bringing new water from the seas to the continents.

Many large cities are so undermined by human mole burrows—traffic tunnels, utility conduits, sewers—that the groundwater level has fallen; this causes the ground to settle, buildings to crack, conduits to break. The ground of some of Stockholm's newly built suburban centers seems already to have sunk by some yards. From the parts of Tokyo most affected by this condition, it is reported that, the ground having sunk four yards in forty years, the high water now washes in over what men have built.

What happens when groundwater is drawn off is that the very earth suffers anemia and hardening of the arteries and shrivels up like the flesh of an old man.

Bewitched by his own technology, man has made himself more and more remote from nature's profound wisdom. Technology is not a demiurge that can create something out of nothing. Technology's accomplishments are merely rearrangements of parts of nature; what it puts into one pocket has to come out of another. The more man's economy replaces nature's, the more violently are elements vital to life gouged out of their natural environment, to be flung into surroundings where they don't belong.

The industrial revolution, new agricultural cultivation methods, and development of sewer-piping and sanitary toilets have seriously distorted certain parts of the cycle. Minerals that should rotate from the soil to the plants, from the plants to the animals, and once again to the soil, are now leached out of the soil and pumped into the waters. All too often our economy becomes a diseconomy.

What is especially ominous is how we are meddling with phosphorus, the cells' fuel. It is far too important for life on land for it to be flung out to nourish blue-green algae or to be deposited in the sea's bottom sediments. Every year three and a half million tons of phosphorus are thus washed out of the earth and dumped into the sea. Even so small a body of water as the Baltic Sea must annually accept enough phosphorus to fill seven hundred railroad cars.

Nutrition experts have warned that phosphorus could become the first of life's vital substances to run out. Someone has remarked that a shortage of phosphorus may be the crisis that will compel man to mine the sea bottom. Perhaps technology will be able to solve that little problem—but the solution will truly be a triumphal step backward.

In this unnatural transportation of elements from land to waters, phosphorus keeps company with nitrogen. Under ideal conditions nitrogen from rotting leaves and from the excrement of animals and man (and ultimately from the creatures themselves) should return to the earth, while at the same time the atmosphere should retrieve the nitrogen they give off. But things no longer work this way—not entirely. Increasingly, synthetic fertilizers are poured over croplands and forests to replace what crop cultivation sucks out of the ground. To a high degree, these nutrients are extracted from atmospheric nitrogen. We now bind as much nitrogen in artificial fertilizers as all of the earth's ecosystems fix in their processes.

It has been computed that by the end of the century man will annually extract a hundred million tons of nitrogen out of the air. If you think about the unseen billions of nitrogen atoms that we draw in with every breath, and which have passed through amoebas and dinosaurs and primates ever since life began, you can get some slight impression of the quantities that synthetic fertilizer factories take out of the air. One can no longer be sure that the atmosphere is getting back as much nitrogen as man is squeezing out of it. Nor can anyone predict what might happen if the air's content of nitrogen were significantly diminished.

We still know appallingly little about what the heaped-up nitrogen fertilizer may mean to microscopic life in croplands and forest soils, but there is no shortage of reasons to worry. What is now visible even to the naked eye is how phosphorus and nitrogen, washed out of the soil, are transforming rivers and lakes: the microbial content increases, the water blooms, the oxygen is exhausted, the fish die. The soil is being depleted, the water, overfertilized—sometimes to the point of stench and death. In flagrant cases the lakes' geological aging, which otherwise would take a long period of time, happens right before our eyes. Even a country like Sweden, in global terms sparsely populated and in environmental terms a minor offender, fertilizes its aggregate water area, on the average, four times as much as its land area.

Around the world, pure fresh water is running short. In many places people no longer know how the product of nature tastes; unsuspecting of the overstatement, they call the evil-smelling liquid that issues from faucets "water."

Even worse, in some places mineral fertilization changes the chemistry of the groundwater by sharply increasing the nitrate content. From drinking water, the nitrates can enter the blood and lessen the hemoglobin's ability to transport oxygen to the body's cells. We know, nowadays, that this is especially threatening to younger children.

Flowing waters are nature's great waste-treatment works, the planet's kidneys. In many places, they are overloaded and no longer able to do their duty. That whole sanguine philosophy, that water ought to be able both to accept and transport our wastes, has gone bankrupt. With a production system that has broken away from the biological system and with an increasingly elaborate throwaway economy, we produce more and more waste that sooner or later ends up in the water: heavy metals, trace elements, biocides. Every year four hundred new chemical substances are produced in the United States alone. Sooner or later, most of them find their way—with untested biological effects—into the water.

The planet's rivers have, to a great extent, been transformed into sewers. Many lakes, clear a generation ago, are so sick today that they may already be beyond redemption.

The greatest profligates with our common capital of soil and water are the big cities. They act as enormous leaks through which earth's riches run out. Once they have soiled their nearest surroundings, they often try to get away from it all by sending their "wastes" out to sea through huge culverts. This solves no problems, merely defers them. Theft from the earth does not grow less because the stolen goods are thrown some distance away. Moreover, the sea has its own vulnerable balance, and in many places we are approaching the limits of the sea's ability to cleanse itself. There are no tubs so large that they can't be dirtied.

The Baltic Sea has experienced suffocation—just as a person will if he cannot get oxygen. Its deeps are, periodically, lifeless deserts where oxygen has been replaced by hydrogen sulfide. The North Sea is used by its coastal countries as a giant cesspool into which the excretions of millions of people are spilled without chemical purification, and into which specially built ships dump hundreds of thousands of tons of the cities' sewer slime and industrial poisons; at times it seems indeed to be a wine-dark sea. Not redness of dawn but dead plankton and residues of vinyl chloride are the cause; dumped in the North Sea, such residues can spread as far as Spitzbergen. Far out to sea float fish poisoned by chlorinated hydrocarbons.

"The sea smiles with its enticing calm, its deceptive stillness," wrote Lucretius, in his great poem of natural philosophy. The sea's glittering calm has become deceptive in a new way: it conceals a multitude of coliform bacteria and other things dangerous to higher life forms. Less poetically than Lucretius, a UNESCO report tells how the waters at a row of swimming resorts along the edge of Normandy and Brittany, the Riviera, and Italy's five thousand-mile coast are so infected that swimmers risk allergic reactions, skin inflammations, and general poisoning. Of Italian coastal waters, only thirteen and a half percent are free of symptoms, thirty-five percent are definitely poisoned, and eighteen percent are dangerous to health. In the last category are found several of the resorts that sun-thirsty northerners most faithfully visit.

Oil spills are going to become a global pollution. The route between the English Channel and the Persian Gulf is so strewn with oil patches that people make the gloomy joke that one can navigate by them—the compass is superfluous. Oil spreads out over great expanses and breaks down very slowly indeed. It smears beaches and robs the wings of sea birds of their lifting power. When Thor Heyerdahl made his sea voyages with *Ra* he found the sea so full of gobs of oil that sometimes it was impossible to bathe—in mid-Atlantic!

The saddest aspect of all this is that our relations with our own original environment are changing. No longer can we approach the sea openly, with a feeling of exhilaration. The currents of the primordial sea that have timelessly rolled through our unconscious mind now freeze in their motion. A kind of wariness, a kind of constraint, a new strangeness is arising between man and the sea. Something important has been lost.

In the sea, clouds of microscopic plants drift unseen by the human eye. These phytoplankton are vital for man and for animal life in general because they are responsible for seven-tenths of the globe's oxygen production. Many scientists wonder how this production may be affected by the chemical pollution of the oceans. When biocides are found concentrated in the flesh of sea fish, it is pretty certain that their plankton food was poisoned. That DDT threatens photosynthesis in the algae has been clearly established. Similarly, an oil film over the water can have a suffocating effect.

Nevertheless, the engines of man's technology are destroying oxygen in quantities exceeding all the oxygen circulating through animal life. At any moment of the day three thousand jet planes on the wing are burning a hundred thousand tons of oxygen per hour. Someone has computed that Americans are burning more oxygen than is produced on their continent; they get by—thanks to oxygen from the Pacific Ocean. No one knows how long we can go on this way. One thing is clear: should the oceans' tiny oxygen producers go on strike, it is going to threaten the very heart of oxygen-based life.

In the breath of life, a certain balance must prevail between oxygen and carbon dioxide. At the same time that the atmosphere's oxygen level is evidently diminishing, the carbon dioxide content is increasing. Every year the atmosphere is supplied with six billion tons of fossil carbon. Some of this probably returns to the earth and fertilizes croplands and woodlands. The rate, however, is going up. It is thought that up to the time that man got the idea of utilizing energy that the vegetable life of ancient ages had deposited in the earth, the carbon dioxide content of the air remained constant. But it has been established that in this century the carbon dioxide content has already risen by fifteen percent. With idiot haste, we are flinging into the sea of air what the eons have collected in the earth-crust's pockets of oil and seams of coal.

When oil and coal are burned, sulfur dioxide is released into the air. Carbon and sulfur are among the building blocks of life. But in the quantities and in the compounds vomited into the environment by the chimneys of homes and factories and the exhaust pipes of automobiles they become corrosive poisons. The emissions of lead, cadmium, mercury, and other heavy metals are also being incessantly increased, as are the applications of biocides. Poisons threaten from the most unexpected directions. From the friction in automobile braking systems, asbestos sprays into the atmosphere. From space rockets chromium dust drifts down and cyanogen rains down, which, mixed with water, can make poisonous prussic acid.

Coal and sulfur pollution, in particular, leave many visible marks on man's environment. Historic stone sculptures are eaten away as if attacked by leprosy. Steel structures rust as much as four times faster than they should. Every year some two million tons of concentrated sulfuric acid falls in the rain upon the Scandinavian peninsula, threatening sensitive woodlands and lowering the acidity of the lakes to a point at which fish can no longer breathe. Much of this is swept up from the Ruhr where it happens, somehow, that one thrifty factory manager or another turns off what purification equipment does exist as soon as the wind veers to a direction that will carry the sulfuric acid away from his immediate vicinity. In Norway's western rivers it is British industries that threaten the salmon and the trout.

Forests have a wonderful ability to filter dust-choked air. Deciduous trees, moreover, renew their filters annually. Normally, therefore, the air is cleaner in the woods than it is in the open. But now, in many places, the trees' purification plants, too, are breaking down. If you should find your way into groves in the Ruhr district of Germany, you will have to risk being smeared, after only a few yards, with soot and other wastes that have come to rest on trunks and branches; the woods you find there are sick woods. The chestnuts are retreating from the boulevards of Paris, having lost an uneven struggle with automobile exhaust. The pines of Rome are folding up their giant parasols.

Mixed with the pollution of smoke and exhaust is acoustic air pollution—the noise from man's machines. Sonic booms from supersonic military planes have been known to cause tens of thousands of tons of rock to fall from mountains, in the same way that a rifle shot can release an avalanche. Despite mounting opposition, and despite economic problems in the experimental stages, several nations seem to have decided that their "prestige" requires that they produce civilian supersonic transports, SSTs, whose only function will be to hurl some infinitesimal fraction of one percent of the world's population from continent to continent a few hours faster than heretofore. What can we expect on the day they unroll their great spreading carpet of noise? Their recurrent artificial thunderclaps may already have had deeper effects on the globe's organisms than we may now suspect. But that sonic booms can cause foetal damage among animals of the forest and among human beings has already been established.

The atomic age, finally, threatens Terra with a whole new dimension of pollution. When we succeeded in thrusting into the atoms' microcosmos, splitting the hitherto indivisible, it was a triumph of the human brain. It was also the riskiest discovery our restlessly searching race had ever made. Today, man can create a radioactive twin, an isotope, for every chemical element of which earth and its diverse expressions of life are composed.

That a general nuclear war could wipe out all higher forms of life is by now a generally accepted truism. Less is said about the risks of civilian nuclear power. Some of the by-products of nuclear fission can be millions of times more poisonous than any known chemical compound. A single nuclear power plant rated at a million kilowatts contains, toward the end of a single burning cycle, more radioactive waste than that vomited out in all the nuclear weapons tests to date. It has already happened that reactors have leaked, radioactively infected gases and water streaming out. Nowadays the risks are regarded as minimal indeed, but technical failure and human error cannot be entirely prevented. A trivial oversight can have fatal consequences.

There is also the problem of what to do with increasing quantities of radioactive wastes. They must be put somewhere—but where? If they are enclosed in ever-so-strong steel and concrete containers and then sunk in the sea's depths or in abandoned mines, they are still there. Strontium 90 and cesium 137 would have to be stored at least six hundred years before being released to the environment. What a cruel burden on coming generations! Long after we are gone and forgotten, *they* will have the oppressive assignment of watching over *our* leftover threats to life.

And the United States Atomic Energy Commission has established that there is leakage from the containers after only twenty years.

The radioactive isotopes now in the water and the air cannot be fetched back. They are already there, part of the cycle, along with all the other pollutants with which *Homo technicus* is filling his environment.

Mountain wanderer, woods rambler, are you an atavism in search of a vanished purity and peace? Hunting for something that becomes ever harder to rediscover?

The wind, rustling the branches, the wind from the taiga or from the watery hunting ground of the albatross, what is it bringing with it?

The wind is a mighty bearer. It can lift the spores from autumn's toadstools miles high and carry them round the globe. On the back of the wind soil from eroding fields can sail across the oceans. Sand that the wind whirls into the air during desert storms in the Sahara, it drops on the West Indies. Today we know that a multitude of poisonous substances, emitted into the air, can be whipped far and wide by the wind, and dropped far from the original sources.

The oceans' winds, the great currents, act in the same way. Like the atmosphere, they have their low pressure and high pressure: eddies of different magnitudes and rates of flow. Deep eddies extending the length of the ocean depths were discovered only about a decade ago. With the help of currents and eddies the pollutants that are released into a bay, perhaps only into a stream, can be spread over great expanses.

Birds can be winged radioactivity; fish, swimming mercury or DDT. Poisons in the water can probably also be lifted up with the evaporation from the oceans to follow the winds in over the land. The spread of biocides and radiactive substances takes place according to patterns surprising even to biologists with long experience in the difficult work of attempting to predict nature's processes.

The whole biosphere is corroded: air, water, earth. The clouds that empty their vessels over the earth, and the spray-heads that are directed against weeds and harmful insects, douse the earth with alien chemicals that, acting together with the impoverishment of organic material, diminish the soil's bacterial life and thereby its fertility—a slow but unrelenting murder of the soil.

Today, everything living is bound together in a communality of pollution. There is no longer any place on earth where one can be sure of escaping it.

There stands man! It was man that technology was supposed to serve, even at the expense of everything else!

Like every other organism, he is naturally a part of his own surroundings. Disturbance and poisoning in his outer environment mean inescapable disturbance and poisoning in his inner environment. The poisons that have entered the circulation of the air, the water, the soil, the plants, and the animals are finding their way inevitably into his cells too.

The dynamic balance in the life of the cells, which began as a current in the sea, is maintained through thousands of simultaneous processes. Specialized substructures in the cell, organelles, cooperate with each other to preserve life's balance. Yet we know very, very little about how various foreign substances affect the functions of the cells. We do know, however, that mercury is deposited in organelles that serve as the cell's waste treatment plants.

Each cell has its specialized assignment and the cellular structure differs accordingly. Liver cells are built otherwise than nerve cells. On the other hand, human liver cells have the same structure as liver cells in other animals. Of two things, then, we can be pretty sure: environmental poisons ascend the chain of life and will reach us eventually, and when they do, they will affect our insides in much the same way as they affect the insides of our fellow creatures.

With the air we breathe, with the water we drink, with the food we eat—with everything, we are taking in foreign substances with which the body's purification plants cannot always cope. Right now every earthly creature carries strontium 90 in its bone marrow and cesium 137 in its tissues—permanent memories of the superpowers' atomic weapons tests. Nearly every bite of food we eat is peppered with biocides. In 1948 the Swiss scientist Paul Hermann Müller received a Nobel Prize for his discovery of DDT; today, with every newborn citizen of the world getting a dose of DDT along with its mother's milk, often in amounts exceeding the so-called tolerance levels recently established—today, governments are beginning to ban the preparation.

Some years ago, the World Health Organization sounded the alarm after thousands of birds, fish, and seals off England's west coast were poisoned by PCB, which was soon found to be an even more insidious environmental poison than DDT and mercury. PCB is now found in the needles of evergreen forests, in the fish of mountain lakes, in the eggs of birds, and in newborn babies. The Swedish Institute of Public Health examined a thousand food products: not one was entirely free of PCB.

In the right dosage, PCB can cause skin lesions and also, like DDT, liver damage. Asbestos, which does not break down in the human body, is one of the many substances that can cause cancer. Various metals and synthetic preparations can attack the testicle cells, affect sex hormones, cause blood diseases, destroy the bone calcium, break down the kidneys.

Lead can stand as the general example of what happens when foreign metals are released into the environment. When the Romans conquered England they set up a number of workshops for the making of lead drinking cups. Today, more than fifteen centuries later, we can still see the scars of that enterprise, partly in the lead-impregnated skeletal parts in the graves of rich Romans, partly in the meager growth on the poisoned soil where the smelter once stood.

Nowadays lead sifts unceasingly out of automobiles' exhaust pipes, falling on meadows and pastures, woods and gardens along all the main roads, and filling the canyon streets of our great cities. It is in the air, it enters into vegetables and grazing animals. From all these sources it reaches man. The "tiger in your tank" is a far greater threat to man than the killer of the jungles ever was. Doctors tell us that lead can cause permanent damage to the brains of children, who have not yet had a chance to develop their potential. We shall never know of what new Raphael, Einstein, or Goethe human civilization may have been deprived by lead.

Practically all great cities have bad breath. Several of them are almost permanently wrapped in a mustard-colored fog that the biologically active parts of the sunlight find it ever harder to penetrate; the sunlight becomes poorer, the dawn comes later and the dusk, earlier. It is such a murk, with all the foulness of which it is composed, that ever increasing numbers of mankind will be breathing in future.

From autopsies, doctors tell us that while the lungs of the decreasing number of country folk still have a fresh red color, the lungs of city dwellers run to various shades of grey. A report from American public health authorities, a couple of years ago, stated that carbon monoxide poisoning in New York City had reached such a level that it could endanger people's brain functions. How neatly this illustrates the treachery of technology, that child of the human brain!

When soot, exhaust, and other environmental poisons are bound together by the dampness of the air, the result is smog—a global disease of civilization that clothes much of the urbanized world in a true Nessus' shirt. During some smog episodes in New York City people have been warned to stay indoors and to keep the windows shut. In Tokyo, where a million and a half tons of particulate matter rain down every year, the inhabitants were warned, during the heavy smog in the fall of 1970, not to breathe too deeply. Japan's enormously expanding capital city can experience a hundred fifty smog warnings a year; in the districts most affected, policemen must return to their stations every half-hour to breathe pure oxygen.

From the great cities and the industrial areas, the tainted air spreads far afield. Former United States Secretary of Health, Education, and Welfare John Gardner has warned his countrymen that they may have to learn how to live indoors like moles, or to use gas masks, if pollution of the air is not soon controlled. Professor Bernhard Grzimek, an environmental expert consulted by the German Federal Chancellor, suggests that, with continued motorization and industrialization, the air of the European continent is going to be so bad by 1980 that elderly persons, at least, will not be seen outdoors without gas masks.

In Yokkaichi, outside Tokyo, several years ago, one could see schoolchildren playing outside at recess equipped with yellow face-masks that were supposed to protect them against poisoned air.

The hunter's descendants have come a long way from his wilderness.

Generation after generation has labored so that the next might have a better life—industries to transform nature's seemingly limitless resources for man's advantage, roads and ships to carry us nearer other groups of men and to convey our goods, schools to widen our race's garnered knowledge, hospitals to heal our bodies, new and better homes—to be filled with more and more unnecessary things.

Then, one day, we are shocked into the awareness that we tread on poisoned ground, that the air we breathe is fast becoming the poison we breathe, that the rain beating down on the fields and the wind wandering through the groves carry with them invisible enemies. As we wander about with strontium in our marrow and DDT in our body tissues, with lead in our kidneys and anxiety in our hearts, we discover with horror that the price of progress has been stunningly high. Outrageously high.

Even worse than the poisons that are sucked into our cells may be the poison that is dropped into our minds. Something is changing in our relations with our entire surroundings—not only with the sea but with the air and the clouds, the earth and its crops. It has been hard enough to bear the feeling of homelessness that has come from civilization's increased distance from nature. That we can no longer go without mistrust to meet that nature which shapes us is something whose monstrousness we have hardly yet begun to appreciate.

And the sneak attack is directed not only against us who are now living. We know extremely little about what effect recognized and unrecognized environmental poisons may have on the germ plasm. Geneticists tremble before their assumptions—or before their uncertainty. If we burden ourselves with defective genes today, it could take generations for the consequences to reveal themselves. Though we have thought (in our technological nearsightedness) that we were working for the benefit of coming generations, we may actually have been working for their incurable injury.

Maybe the primate who climbed down from the tree has been the greatest natural catastrophe ever suffered by Terra.

Surely it will take not much more to tip over the incredibly delicate balance in the biosphere. It is impossible for us to foresee just when the irreversible event may occur, or what its efficient cause might be. Lack of phosphorus or oxygen? Mangled genes? Or what the meteorologist Morris Neiburger says he fears, a smog that settles round the world, withering man's civilization not through some sudden catastrophe but through a gradual poisoning with the earth's own elements?

In any case, that our course so far has been taking us ever nearer an ecological breakdown cannot be doubted. It is true that the great oxygen catastrophe three billion years ago raised the curtain upon life as it has since developed. But another equally dramatic revolution in the biosphere, caused by one of the earth's life forms, would not open possibilities for new life; it would, instead, close the final curtain on the drama of life on this particular planet.

By poisoning nature and hence ourselves we have introduced something entirely new into evolution. The radical change of course that would enable us to avert a breakdown is made the more difficult by a pair of factors that work like mighty engines behind the destruction of the environment.

Beguiled by his own technology, technical man is constantly driven to pursue increased material growth. If all countries achieved the same living standard as the United States, the earth's atmosphere would be loaded with two hundred times more sulfur than pollutes it now, seven hundred fifty times more carbon monoxide, ten thousand times more asbestos. Rivers, lakes, and seas would have to accept one hundred seventy-five times more chemical poisons. The world's remaining forests would be reduced by two-thirds; this, in combination with the poisoning of the oceans' phytoplankton, would drastically lessen the world's oxygen supply. Soot and dust in the air would screen away more and more of the sunshine.

A tidal wave of prosperity would sweep the globe and soon render it uninhabitable.

To equal the United States' material standard of living is the expressed goal of the Soviet Union, China, and Europe. The underdeveloped countries, without exception, are trying to move in the same direction. Japan, the quickest and most thorough environment destroyer of them all, is trying to excel the United States and will probably do so. As for the Americans themselves, they speak of tripling their already-high living standard by the end of the century.

However, the most serious threat to the environment ultimately lies in man's incessant multiplication.

The biosphere's food resources are limited. Nutritional physiologists seem to be attacked by darker and darker doubts about the very possibility of coping with the doubling of the human species predicted for the year 2000. The sea has not turned out to be the friend-in-need of which we once dreamed. All that talk of its "unlimited" resources has shown itself to be—talk. Only seven percent of the sea's surface is productive—and it is this same seven percent that man is, to an increasing degree, polluting with his wastes.

So it is out of the continents' eroded, exhausted, pesticide-saturated earth that the nourishment must be taken. A chorus of voices from west and east, such as the American biologist Paul Ehrlich and the father of the Russian atomic bomb Andrei Sakharov, predict that within a few decades there will already be gigantic hunger catastrophes with suffering, despair, and violence of such magnitude that they will have profound consequences for everyone on earth. Perhaps the much-heralded Green Revolution with high-yielding crops can delay the dreaded food crises for a bit. But if the population curve continues to climb the reprieve will be a brief one.

Besides, in a somewhat larger perspective, the central question is not simply one of how much food the earth can be made to produce but of the consequences for the biosphere if a single species takes so much for its own share.

The balance of life rests upon multiplicity. Every species has its place in the scheme of things. In a harmonious ecosystem, every species has, besides, a genetic range over which natural selection can play in order to adjust different plants and animals to shfiting environmental conditions. When we have cultivated certain crops and enforced a one-sided choice in the direction of high-yielding domesticated plants, variable and valuable gene material has dropped out that otherwise we would be able to build upon in new situations. This has already meant a permanent impoverishment of the biosphere.

Through his disproportionate numerousness, man is now suppressing more and more other creatures in the great scheme. Links that break—animals that are exterminated, plants that disappear—can never more be replaced. This could have consequences for the global ecosystem just as profound as those of the irresponsible manipulation of nature's variable elements.

A creature that triumphs too completely in the struggle for existence puts himself in danger. The hunter depends upon his quarry. Where no quarry remains, there is no longer any place for a hunter.

Perhaps we are already too many. We can quickly become many too many.

7

How many things the men of future ages shall know, which are unknown to us . . . although the nature of things does not give up its secret all at once. We think ourselves admitted to the sanctum, but we find that we are only in the outermost chambers.
Linnaeus, *On Wonder Before Nature*

THE BRAIN IS LIKE A WOOD. If you look at a section of the brain under magnification you can easily imagine that you are standing before a confusing multitude of strangely shaped exotic trees, some with high trunks, spreading crowns, and sparse branches; others gently interlaced with leafy branchwork; still others crowded together in tight thorny thickets.

In a real wood, the trees' root systems are joined with one another so that water, nourishing substances, and poisons can spread, by way of the roots, from tree to tree. Mirroring this, the branches come together, touch each other, intertwine.

In the same way, branches and roots in the forest of the brain plait themselves one into another in a bewildering tangle of innumerable connection lines and contact points. Under the microscope, the brain section is like a fascinating but impenetrable jungle.

In the forest of his own brain, man has lost his way. This brain has garnered into its fourteen billion cells ever more, ever greater, ever riskier knowledge. But our knowing has remained divided and disconnected. We have been unable to collect ourselves, to achieve that commanding grasp of our knowledge that would be the sign of wisdom.

One can imagine, sometimes, that man has been the victim of the most pitiless of evolution's many paradoxes. His mind has developed to such a degree that he is technologically capable of making radical transformations in his physical surroundings—and he exercises that capability. At the same time, however, thinking himself separate from the rest of nature, he uses his talents in ways that threaten the very foundations of his own existence.

And now we are about to pick even more inaccessible and perhaps even bitterer fruits from the tree of knowledge. The technological revolution that has burst upon us in the last generation was long and slowly prepared. Now our slow biological evolution is about to turn, just as abruptly, into a biological revolution.

The heralds who have foretold this have barely been able to make themselves heard, or else they have not been taken seriously. What the English writer Gordon Rattray Taylor has called the "biological time bomb" can find us as unprepared as the people of Hiroshima when the atomic bomb was dropped on them.

No longer satisfied with manipulating our external environment, we are beginning to manipulate ourselves. We are approaching the climax of evolution, when a species can consciously change itself and thereby take the responsibility for its own continued evolution. Not the powers that we have conjured out of the hearts of the atoms, nor the spacecraft with which we are beginning to fill the silent interplanetary voids, are likely to be more decisive for our race than the step before which we are poised. Our thirst for knowledge and our curious probing into nature having led us toward the solution of the riddles of life and death, we ourselves step forward in the role that we formerly assigned to the gods we had created in our own image.

When one considers the harm we have done to our surrounding environment (generally without knowing it), one shudders to think of the uses to which our new biological discoveries may be put before we have won through to sufficient certitude and wisdom. It can be difficult to distinguish use and misuse; what begins as a blessing can as easily become a curse.

Biological evolution, controlled by natural selection, is about to become biological revolution in four areas. These are: transplantation of organs, postponement of death, genetic control, and personality modification, chiefly accomplished through manipulation of the brain.

Of the four, transplantation is the only one really reflected in the headlines. Up to the end of the 1960s the transplantation specialists were mainly occupied with transplanting kidneys, but in just a few years a number of heart transplants have been carried out in the limelight. Most have failed. But behind the headlines, in the laboratories and out of the limelight, the surgeons have solved most of the technical problems of transplanting the liver, lungs, and other internal organs.

Surely the first organ-banks are about to be established, where deep-frozen organs will be stored as spare parts for human machines that break down. Human organs can be complemented with organs from our nearest related species: ape farms may come to be established whose whole mission will be to supply people with healthy organs, just as our chicken farms supply us with eggs and broilers, and our dairy barns with milk and beefsteaks. New industries will probably grow up, too, for the manufacture of artificial arteries, heart valves, and kidneys, and perhaps for complete signal systems that will sound the alarm if something malfunctions. Damaged people can also be patched up with new limbs; Chinese and Japanese surgeons seem already to have succeeded in transplanting hands and feet.

That surgery can replace separate worn-out or injured organs of an otherwise healthy individual means a humanitarian advance that no one would wish to give up. The crux of the matter is simply this: once we have mastered the technique of exchanging parts, there will no longer be a point where we can say thus-far-no-further. An advanced transplant technique could change our ways of thinking quite a lot. Perhaps it will come to be regarded as primitive, prejudiced, and economically irresponsible to bury organs together with their original owner. Perhaps the dying will be thought to have a duty to bequeath any of their organs that are not worn out. When a man comes to consist more and more of potential spare parts, the old questions of personal identity will come sneaking back, almost imperceptibly, along entirely new paths.

This will be trifling, however, compared with the consequences of our being able, through repeated exchange of organs or through chemical methods, to extend man's life span or, anyway, to postpone his death. The new chemistry, especially, contains possibilities it is hard to see to the end of. Chemistry builds up, chemistry dissolves. Death proceeds from the collapse of the separate cells as a consequence of chemical reactions. It has been learned that if one takes aged cells from a man and places them in a suitable nutrient solution, they are revitalized. It is said that certain soil bacteria, among other things, might block cell decay. Biologists are beginning to speak hopefully of being able to create new editions of Methuselah, yes, even of being able to realize the old dreams of immortality. Suffice it to say that, even before the end of this century, we are going to be able to extend the life span by some decades.

It is here that the real problems begin. Even if man overcomes his fear of death, he is not very likely to stop leaping at possibilities of lengthening his life. The result could be a hypochondriacal poking into organs and messing around with potions. And if there should not be enough to go around, who gets to live, who must die? The doctors of tomorrow may face appalling decisions. They—or perhaps the collectivity, the community.

But perhaps we have a clock built into us that regulates our life cycle. If so, a postponed death could become an extended senility. Is it with such matters that the industrialized nations shall trifle, while the underdeveloped nations starve and become overpopulated? And what kind of spiritual climate can prevail in a society overweighted on the side of (perhaps apathetic) old people? Postponing death could become one of the greatest ironies ever prepared by man for himself. Taylor has pointedly reminded us that it was precisely immortality that was the punishment imposed upon Ahasuerus, the Wandering Jew, for his refusal to let Jesus rest at his house on the way to Golgotha.

Even more bewildering are the possibilities of interceding in the processes of inheritance and deciding our own genetic future, just as we now do with some of our crop plants and domestic animals.

Artificial insemination is already routine. Sperm banks, where prospective mothers could order sperm with guaranteed genetic qualities, could become as common as blood banks. In principle, sperm can be deep-frozen for as long as you like: A man now living might beget children a thousand or ten thousand years hence. Looking at it from another perspective, it is as if a woman should today choose to have a child by Columbus or Caesar. A fertilized ovum can be implanted in the womb of a foster mother, who gives the child her blood but not her characteristics. From here it is not a very big step to artificial wombs, or to the embryo in the test-tube. All this could change our view of the role of the family.

So far we have been discussing fertilization, albeit fertilization in a manner somewhat different from nature's. The breaking of the genetic code opens up other and still wider possibilities. It has given us new understanding of how the mechanism of inheritance functions. To understand is to be able to intervene and to change. Working with genes and chromosomes, genetic engineers can transfer characteristics from one individual to another. One can alter the message of the living cell so as to accomplish specified results. This is no longer a matter of transplanting to modify single individuals, but of altering, eventually, the whole species.

So long as the new (and still incomplete) discoveries about DNA were used to eliminate inherited defects, perhaps to prevent cancer and diabetes or possibly to avert some of the effects of the poisoning of our environment, these discoveries might be blessings. But if they were carried further? Our vision falters.

It is generally recognized nowadays that the medical and hygienic progress that has softened the harshness of natural selection has also led to a weakening of the human race that may have snowballing consequences in the next century. Guiding man's development back on the track may come to be regarded as necessary. If so, choosing between genes to be thrown out and genes to be carried further will be a fateful question indeed.

There is also serious discussion of drawing together, in a human breeding "stable," persons with special aptitudes for particular tasks such as space travel. It would even be possible for individual genes with special value to be carried across the boundary of the species. Nothing indicates that man has become more intelligent since Cro-Magnon. Now the possibility is discussed of bringing forth supermen with extremely high intelligence quotients: a new aristocracy, genetically developed. The transplant men regard it as possible to make real those chimera, beings midway between man and beast, that the fantasies of antiquity glimpsed in the darkness of the woods. In the same vein, the gene engineers talk about the possibility of creating a new race through crossing genes over the species boundary. By comparison, the race problems we have had up to now could pale into insignificance.

Another and even more curious possibility could arise from cloning, whereby a single cell is made to produce thousands and hundreds of thousands of doubles of itself, just as amoeba do. So far men have succeeded in cloning only some domestic plants and certain lower organisms. But there is ample reason to believe that we will be able to make human clones someday. On that day a man will be able, in effect, to have himself born anew, see himself grow up again, and fill the surroundings with his own multiplication—a wish fulfilment for Narcissus, a nightmare for others.

The realization of many of these partly astonishing, partly frightening, possibilities may be nearer than most people suspect. James Danielli, a British biologist who has worked on assembling new artificial cells out of parts of living cells, predicts that in about ten years men will already be able to give simple cells extra genes and chromosomes; in twenty years, make synthetic mammals, even such mammals as nature has never seen before; and, at a somewhat later date, make synthetic men.

Much is becoming possible for us, it seems, but not every possibility is good for us. All the mistakes that have led to the poisoning of our external environment we have made because we did not know what nature would stand for. Still less can we expect nature to reveal all her secrets the moment we shoulder our way into her innermost chambers. Advantages won in one direction could be counterbalanced by risks from another. Through carelessness, valuable genetic material could be lost forever. Mistakes could lead to changes in the species that would first emerge in generations yet to come.

Just as two-edged are those discoveries with which we are trying to act upon the vegetation of our brain—that peculiarly soft clump, weighing hardly more than two pounds, nature's most complicated production, the organ of "psychic metabolism," the workshop of consciousness and knowing, whose chemical processes, mostly concealed from us, generate the electrical twenty-watt effect in which thoughts and images arise.

Classical brainwashing—inspired by Pavlov's famous dog experiments, successfully practiced by our century's dictators, and capable of breaking down the strongest personality beyond recognition—already seems antiquated by comparison with the more sophisticated electrical and chemical methods now being developed.

That living creatures can be electrically manipulated is considered a very real possibility. By inserting fine electrodes into the brain, one can activate its different centers. By this method, for example, apes have been caused to experience intense sexual pleasure. Learning which lever released the electrical impulse, the apes have pressed it themselves, time after time, in order to experience the pleasure. On the other hand, it has been possible to kill apes through electromagnetic oscillations corresponding to the brain's own oscillation rate. Between these extremes lies a broad spectrum of possibilities.

Chemistry probably opens up an ever lengthening list of influences, through substances that are either injected directly into the brain or conveyed to it by the bloodstream. That various kinds of illness can be cured chemically is one of the blessings of medicine. Perhaps it may also be beneficial if inhibited natures can be made more open, and aggressive ones made more peaceful. But how long can we continue to manipulate the vital center of the personality without doing damage to the human mind? When one has seen the way that the biocides man uses against "pests" in nature rebound against man himself, one has reason to fear what may happen if we blunder heedlessly into the mind's fragile and poorly explored labyrinths.

And the step from use to planned abuse is very short. To remote-control people's moods could—indeed, would—become a dictator's chemistry. It is probably a no more difficult feat to force-feed a community's citizens by putting a submission drug in the community water supply than it is to give them fluorides to prevent dental caries.

It is now believed that memory springs from chemical processes. The memory can be chemically activated or suppressed. But evidently it should also be possible to inject memory transferred from other persons or brought clear over the boundary of the species from other animals, since it appears that memory in all living things may be based upon identical codes. Even if this should never happen with people—with animals it is already being tested—it reminds us what power we are on the way toward usurping to ourselves.

We have reached a stage of evolution at which we can change identities and create human beings without identity.

In nearly every field, man's increased knowledge has brought him to a crossroads. The inscriptions on the signposts are gloomy ones.

The wanderer in the autumn woods hears the wind strike up a tune. It snatches a few leaves from the ground and whirls them toward him; the setting sun gives them a fleeting luster. The wind, the leaves, the sun that sinks toward the horizon, all carry with them timeless, unprogramed messages. Wordlessly, they sink deep into the wanderer.

In the technological society genuine, unprogramed messages are the fewer, artificial, programed ones the more numerous—fabricated by experts who know how the human psychology functions and are ambitious to transmit a maximum impression in a minimum of time. Tomorrow's most important message center may well be the synthetic brains that increasingly complement and also, to some still unknown degree, compete with the human brain.

Computers represent something so decisively new in the development of human civilization that they can only be compared with the discovery of written language. But while writing was developed slowly, new generations of computers follow close upon one another. They are going to reach deep into our ways of living together. They will come to be used not only for community and industrial planning, long-range weather forecasting, medical diagnosis, and various research applications, but even in the home. Perhaps before the end of the century they will be as common and as indispensable as the telephone or the radio. The products that one has chosen on the television screen (rather than in the shop) will be ordered and paid for by computer. Above all, a revolutionizing portion of our flood of information is going to be flowing through the computer.

What this may mean ultimately we can only begin to suspect. Perhaps we may become as dependent on the computer as we are on the spoken and written word. Doors could open to worlds of information that would enrich the individual's existence in ways presently unknown. But the computer might also lull us. We could come to depend more and more upon the computer memory, less and less upon our own. We could come to depend more and more on the computer's judgment, too.

However, the whole mass of information that man has garnered since the art of writing was discovered can never be stored in a computer center. Nor can more than a fraction of what we are today producing be so stored. A selection must be made. This imposes an enormous responsibility upon those who do the selecting. Here too the step from use to abuse is all too short, the consequences enormous. New class distinctions could arise between those who have free access to information and those who merely get programed. An all-embracing computer system, which also had all relevant data on private persons stored in its memory, could become a dictator's tool in the same way as the brain drugs could.

The present generation of computers is considered to have only a tenth of man's intelligence quotient. But while man's intelligence has long remained the same, the computer's increases incessantly. There are technologists who look forward to computers with IQs superior to man's. Perhaps they will not go that far. But it is easy enough to imagine computers, with their capacity to provide rapid and emotionless answers to complicated questions, becoming the decisive factor in many situations and attaining thereby a de facto position of power that we could not previously have imagined. When the day comes that computers can intervene in every aspect of daily life, when their synthetic intelligence can solve problems before which man himself vacillates, when—perhaps—they can program themselves and give instructions that man cannot understand, this could give rise to a collective feeling of powerlessness. What that might imply for a species that has believed itself master of creation by virtue of the power of its brain is not easy to predict.

In the future of biology and technology are glimpsed possibilities of a symbiosis between man and machine. A cybernetic organism (a "cyborg," to use the jargon name for such a centaur of the technological age) is, in a way, a logical next step in development. Every machine, even the simplest, increases human muscle power and thereby enlarges the capabilities granted man by nature. But when man creates machines, he has to adapt himself to their environment. The Industrial Revolution forced its servants to adapt their bodily and, to a great extent, their psychological rhythms to the mechanical motions of the machines.

Development proceeds. Rushing along the roads encapsulated in our cars, we have fused with our metal shells almost like the snail with his snailshell. The astronaut, traveling through the reaches of space, has proceeded several degrees further: symbiotically, he is united with his capsule, an integral part of its technical and ecological microworld. Surgeons' increased ability to unite protoplasm and synthetic components means, eventually, a step toward the union of man and machine.

Bright-eyed biotechnologists now fantasize about being able to couple a computer and a human brain. Surgeons who have dissected out the brains of rhesus monkeys and bathed them with blood (to oxygenate the cells) have succeeded in keeping such brains alive for as long as eighteen hours. Perhaps such a brain can think, perhaps it can remember—no one knows whether it can also feel pain. In any case, it seems to react to noise. In some cases the brain was removed along with an eye; when light was directed at the pupil, the iris contracted. In the context of such experiments we can visualize a theoretical possibility of connecting human and synthetic intelligence directly. A biological computer—that would be an example of man/machine symbiosis both apt and macabre!

The computer serves to illustrate the mighty, almost self-activating power that growth and change have become in modern man's society.

In all social systems, growth is a magical concept. Holy, holy, holy is the name of Gross National Product; governments, legislatures, and organizations are its prophets. To question why or whether GNP ought to be raised three or four percent every year is to verge on blasphemy.

Growth means that an ever swifter stream of things gushes forth from the machines. To keep the growth process from being interrupted, new needs must continually be created and things must be thrown away almost as quickly as they are produced. Ten years from now, it has been estimated, half the things on the market will be such as are not even produced today. If things are not replaced by new ones, they must at least be given a new design, be made "up-to-date." Things have progressively shorter lifetimes, are tossed out sooner, and pile up higher at the garbage dumps—the pyramids of our time. The British philosopher Alfred North Whitehead pointed out that the greatest innovation of the industrial era has been "the discovery of discovery itself." The new is accorded a value unto itself, changes are desired and accepted for their own sake. A large part of society's resources are invested in persuading people that they must choose among the things being produced today and reject what was produced yesterday.

This is affecting the continuity of our lives. The things with which we surround ourselves do more than serve their specific purposes. We develop relationships with the things we use for a long time. In a special way, they stabilize life. Maybe it is simply that we preserve some part of our identity through them. Leaving aside the fact that the "growth" society's economy means an irresponsible waste of the earth's limited resources, our entire way of experiencing life becomes shallower and more uneasy when things merely pass by.

The winds of change are blowing with mounting force everywhere in our environment. Probably the landscape now changes more quickly in a generation than it formerly did in a thousand years. In the great cities, large sections are continually being torn down in order to make way for the new. The buildings in a modern city are shells that are not expected to last more than thirty-five years. Excavations of demolished blocks are almost the only permanent features of the central city. No city plan remains firm; every city is an ongoing remodeling process. It is getting harder and harder to find a familiar view on which to rest your eyes.

Automatic data processing, automation, and robots can also fundamentally change man's role in the production process. Like so much else, this trend can be a two-edged blade. Communications of various kinds may become nearly as important as production. Increased specialization and unceasing innovation may force the individual to make frequent changes of profession, a series of careers, with all that this implies by way of breaking with routine and learning new ways to operate. Speed has conquered distance; change of residence can also become more and more common. All this can lead to our relations with other people becoming as temporary, as fragmentary, as our relations with everyday objects.

The road of life is going to be marked by tighter and tighter turns, each affecting our experience of our surroundings, our sense of time, our entire psyche.

The future is invading the present. We attempt to interpret its signs, follow its trends. But we can never know how the man of tomorrow is going to experience his world. To him, much may seem acceptable, and "given," that we find alarming, disturbing, even repulsive.

One of the most constant features of man's nature is his adaptability. He became a specialist in nonspecialization and this has brought him through many vicissitudes. He has made it this far by being the most mobile of all the creatures in a natural world where nothing is static, where everything is change, renewal, evolution. But even man's ability to adapt is not unlimited. The chemistry of the body has not changed since we climbed down from the trees, and our deeper instincts and needs haven't changed much, either. Should the changes all around us become too quick, we are going to find ourselves further and further out of touch with nature's rhythm. A limit does exist, however elastic, beyond which not even strength of will can adapt to the incessant acceleration.

The continual need to adjust oneself to new situations in which one is unsupported by experience and routine, to play new roles, and to obey the rushing torrent of programed messages—all this can disturb what inner balance perchance remains. As Alvin Toffler wrote, this is as if a recording of a funeral march were played at too high a speed: nothing distinct, nothing over which to linger, nothing to touch your heart, only a merry tinkle of sounds.

If you move a tree from its original surroundings to another place, be it ever so suitable, the tree will stop growing unless you bring along with it a clump of the old surroundings, in the form of a goodly ball of earth round the roots. Should you move it repeatedly, the tree will never have time to take root and will wither.

It is not much different with man. The restless changing of the globe is destroying much on which his nature has depended for millions of years. Being constantly tossed about deprives him of intimacy with life, of having a place in a community, of being part of life's own rhythm.

All this can come to exert a grinding pressure, equivalent to the most sophisticated brainwashing. Carried to extremes, it could lead to a collective mental collapse.

The harder the man-created pressure on the environment, the more difficulty man has in escaping it. He has more and more to escape from, and a harder and harder time finding a refuge anywhere.

Even in John Stuart Mill's day a world from which solitude was banished seemed a poor prospect. He meant the fruitful solitude in which a man can enter his own inner space. We are now on the way to a mass society in which man is deprived of his private space. Creative and experience-filled solitude is being replaced by an empty solitariness. It is caused by the cutting of the fine threads of familiarity that exist among men in smaller communities. It leads to the individual's becoming an atom in a monotonous, impersonal collectivity.

There are futurologists who predict that the global population in the year 2100 will total somewhere between twenty to fifty billion people, and that ninety percent of them are going to be living in one more or less continuous urban system, an Ekumenopolis, occupying all the coasts of the world. Such a prospect should alone suffice to make one decline all officious invitations to personal immortality.

Matters need not go nearly that far before the globe becomes a place from which silence and peace of mind will have been driven, where the sky is hardly ever free of flying objects, and where man can no longer find the living space, the seclusion, the sense of distance that his deeply rooted biological instincts demand. The situation that we have inflicted on some of our nearest relations, those we have imprisoned in crowded zoos where stress and shock break down the animals' territorial patterns and thereby their normal social patterns—this is the situation we are fast creating for ourselves.

Our gnawing mistrust of our environment, where poisons threaten us from constantly new directions; our dread of what our intruding into the sanctums of life may mean for our species; the harder and harder hammering of the growth-, change-, and crowd-societies upon our minds—all these things together threaten to eject us into a homelessness more terrible than any faced by humankind before. We are going to be as uprooted as the forests from which, long since, we came.

Still, we must believe that somewhere beyond the covering underbrush and the tangling thicket in the woods of our brain there is a path of wisdom—the path we need to find, for life's sake!

But it seems a long way off. Longer than long.
And time is short.

8

> *Didst thou imagine*
> *That I should detest existence,*
> *Flee into the desert,*
> *Because not all*
> *Dreams i' th' bud grew flowers?*
> Goethe, *Prometheus*

THE WORLD-TREE SWAYS.

    For billions of years it grew ring upon ring. Species glided into its shadow and vanished again, while the tree's growth remained barely perceptible. Suddenly, after ages of gradual development, it seems to burst the vault of heaven; the crown swells illimitably, the branches shoot up farther and farther into space and are caught in the cosmic wind, while the roots, clasping that little shred of space where once the tree began to sprout, seem ever less secure.

    A wanderer, only lately arrived, who lingers a moment at the foot of the tree, seems to hear a raucous echo of the sibyl's prophecy:

> *Yggdrasil trembles, the towering ash*
> *Groans in woe . . .*

Is it the winds of the cosmic autumn that are tearing at the world-tree's crown and threatening to wrench the roots from their mooring?

Or . . .

All around, on dark points in the universe, the possibilities of mind that exist in the cosmic material surely must have taken shape in intelligent beings. All around us, on worlds that shall always remain unknown to us, such beings may reach a critical point in their own development.

They need not be cast in the same mold as we. Life may partly have chosen other elements as its basis. Development may have followed other paths. Their minds may function in other ways than ours do.

But it must be part of the essence of intelligence to search, to experiment, to try to use a planet's resources for the purposes of the species. Before insights into the scheme of things have ripened—and such insights are won, as a rule, through experiences dearly bought—increased technological ingenuity must lead almost automatically to rearrangements in nature that disturb original balances and that ultimately may threaten life itself. An intelligence that has reached a certain level may also be driven by an inner force (in which one may suspect a cosmic logic) to intrude into life's and matter's innermost chambers, with all the risks that that entails for the organism and for its planetary home.

We can assume that innumerable planetary civilizations have gone under because the intelligent beings have not mastered their crisis of development. But there should also exist a number of other worlds where intelligence did manage to cross the critical threshold. Where this has happened, great possibilities for continued development must have opened up.

The drama must surely have been played out again and again through eternities long past, and it is surely being performed in countless places in the universe in the relative present.

If this is the planetary situation that confronts us after billions of years of preparation, then, truly, space arches high above our fate.

We stand at a crossroads in the history of our species. In a special way it is like the crossroads at which the primate stood when he was compelled to leave his tree existence. And yet it is also quite unlike any previous experience of the species. While the creature who had been driven from his home in the trees had millions of years in which to adjust to new and danger-filled surroundings, we have been thrown by violently accelerated technological development into a situation in which we must make our choice with the utmost quickness and must choose deliberately, not haphazardly as always before. It was during the last generation that our civilization reached the critical threshold. We may have but a single generation in which to gain control over our collective conduct and to keep our world from becoming one of those where evolution tested the possibilities of mind—and failed.

We are moving over the narrowest isthmus of time, guided by knowledge bursting with risks. We can no more quit ourselves of it than we can leap over our own shadows. Individuals may spurn development, species cannot. The relevant question is, how we make use of our knowledge.

An intelligent being who gradually increases his resources of knowledge probably always runs the risk of being so impressed by how much he knows that he loses sight of how much he doesn't know at all. Limited knowledge and limitless ignorance are equally responsible for man's predicament. Now, when we are on the way to becoming the victims of our own successes, we have had an almost electrifying reminder of our knowledge's limitations. We have discovered how easily mistakes can be made. We begin to suspect that in the future even the slightest mistakes may have catastrophic consequences.

Up to now we have used our knowledge to try to

"master" nature. We cannot accomplish this, and we are beginning to realize it. The test that remains is to try to master ourselves.

In this corner of the universe man is the only being who knows that an evolution is going on. This is knowledge newly won, hardly more than a century old. Through that knowledge, our existence has gained a perspective for the first time.

Man is also the only being who can affect his own evolution, and that knowledge is a child of the present generation. He has reached a stage at which he not only can but must take the responsibility for his own continued development and for his planet home. The obligation to do this was the price of his knowledge. There is no way back.

This above all makes it impossible to compare our predicament with any other in the history of life—life on this particular heavenly body.

The realization that this is so may call forth feelings of both desolation and humility. Desolation because man, at his crossroads, must recognize with aching clarity that, in his weakness and perplexity, he has no one else to lean on and seek direction from. Humility because evolution has elected his species, out of the myriad of life forms, to undergo the planetary test.

Earth has been furrowed and scarred since it was handed over to the genus Homo. But our solar system should still have billions of years ahead of it, before our sun disintegrates. As a new arrival among the species, man ought to consider that he is at the beginning of his development, provided he can save himself from himself. This presupposes that he is equal to the task of changing this period of seething conflict and anxiety into what the Swedish-American Nobel laureate Glenn Seaborg spoke of as "a period of unprecedented maturity."

To enable our species to have the chance to guide its own continued evolution, we need immediately to straighten out certain elementary relations with our terrestrial surroundings. We need to combine our anxiety and our intelligence, our will and our exertions, into an immediate global crisis program.

Its first commandment ought to read: Prevent by abstention! There are discoveries that man would best exploit, if possible not at all, or if necessary only with the utmost care, because in some cases he now knows the ecological consequences, and in other cases he cannot yet assess them.

No one doubts that our technical men are now able to divert rivers, or currents in the sea; they need not prove it. On the other hand, they cannot predict the effects of such a diversion upon the climate and so it is better that they abstain. When we know that seven-tenths of all the particles in the air of the cities are unidentified and that their biological effects are unknown, it makes more sense to find out the effects of the substances already there than it does to dump new synthetic substances into the environment. When you can already travel between the hemispheres in a few hours, there is no pressing necessity to befoul the atmosphere further with SSTs' sonic booms. When clean and unlimited sources of energy from fusion power are said to be within reach, maybe before the end of the century, one ought to be extremely cautious about increasing the planet's layer of radioactive fallout. Our newly acquired possibilities to affect the life processes ought to be utilized with tremendous discretion and restraint—above all, when we begin to meddle with the drop that contains mankind's genetic inheritance.

The next commandment ought to be: Stop the pursuit of excessive growth, which strains both our minds and our surroundings and means, in many cases, robbing future generations. What drove us out upon this hunt for progress that can put an end to progress?

A theory intrudes and demands to be examined. Perhaps growth frenzy, with its hunger for things, goes back to a mechanism that was developed during those ages when the man-primate lived a hard and threatened life, always on the edge of starvation. When the elemental struggle for existence demanded the harnessing of every muscle and nerve to the requirements of survival, anything that man acquired over and above the bare necessities must have seemed especially desirable and valuable. This genetically programed craving followed us into the affluent society, with its many artificial needs. If this theory is correct, we are dealing with inherited attitudes that once served survival but, themselves surviving, have come to work against their original function.

We cannot establish a moratorium on innovation. So long as there are men on earth, technology will continue to develop. Fibrous materials may be produced that are many times stronger and more workable than steel. With increased knowledge of how nature works, man may learn to imitate the chlorophyll-green miracle in the leaves' extraordinarily efficient food factories. But no innovation can free man from the necessity of drawing his raw material out of this planet, which is (from the standpoint of our housekeeping) a closed storeroom with limited supplies. Our desire for growth must be subordinated to our overriding need for balance. In area after area, we need to check our situation and apply the brakes—before a catastrophe, with conclusive effectiveness, does so for us.

The third and inescapable commandment must be to reinstate, so far as possible, nature's own order.

We cannot consume anything. Only for a short time may we make use of what we take from nature. What once has served our economy we speak of as "waste" to be thrown away. Nature knows no "waste," only circulation, and on a shrinking globe there is no longer any "away." The earth has become our nest, we the only creature that fouls its own nest. What we need now is a comprehensive plan for geohygiene.

If the earth is to continue to be capable of production, then the minerals that we now heave into the water, after a short loan, must be restored to the soil. Metals and chemicals that we use in our homes and factories must be reused again and again and again. What we prodigally regard as waste must be put into a continual cycle of production/utilization/return—in imitation of nature. Reprocessing works must become one of the future's essential industries. Simultaneously, we must resolutely stop continued pollution, and attempt, so far as possible, to decontaminate our environment—especially in the case of persistent chemicals that eat their way into living organisms. It may take several generations before man can tolerably restore what the generations now living have destroyed. The biosphere can probably never regain its original purity. We must reduce our ambition down to creating the greatest possible measure of relative purity.

Nothing in this crisis program would constitute a step forward! All it could accomplish would be to enable our species, having perceived the danger, to jump aside—as instinct causes a person to do when he is about to be run over. It is a minimum program with the limited aim of making continued development possible.

However, one need only imagine every citizen's being assured by law of the elementary right not to be imposed upon by the dross leavings of other people's activities—imagine his being guaranteed the *right* to clean air, to quiet, to solitude—to see how an immediate crisis program would shake up the economic and productive foundations of our present system. We ought not allow ourselves any illusions. It is not likely that even a minimum program to assure the continuation of the species will be feasible except at the cost of simultaneous and profound changes in man's attitudes and institutions.

It is now a commonplace to say that every attempt to stop destruction of the environment is going to flop if mankind cannot at the same time be induced to halt its own growth. Even here we probably run into a deep-seated biological attitude. Until quite recently few children ever reached maturity; natural selection weeded mankind as heavily as it did the other forms of life. Keeping the birth rate a little ahead of infant mortality was a biological contest. When medical progress later lowered the death rate, the old pattern survived—sometimes justified by social or religious doctrines—in the form of resistance to limiting births—another example of how an attitude that was once life sustaining can work to precisely the opposite effect in a different set of circumstances.

Man's numbers must be viewed primarily in relation to earth's supportive capacity. The pressure on earth's resources is already far too great. Were all earth's inhabitants to be given the living standard presently enjoyed by the people of the highly industrialized nations, earth would be able to accommodate only a third of its present population. Man will doubtless find ways—new sources of energy, new methods of production—by which to feed more people than can be fed now. One is reluctant, however, to regard mankind as a mass that blindly expands and expands, like a bacterial culture, until the exhaustion of nutrients sets a limit to its number. Sheer quantity can also come into serious conflict with man's values and dignity. A *decent* human existence must be an existence without crowding—and space cannot be created.

We need to seek certain generally acceptable criteria for a living standard that permits man to live, not merely exist, during the few cosmic seconds allotted to our kind—criteria that include not merely freedom from hunger and deprivation but also protection of air, water, and soil, and the preservation of man's quiet and his *room to live*. From such a starting point an attempt should be made to define an optimum population, and all resources—technical, medical, legal, and educational—should be devoted to the difficult and delicate task of modifying imprinted patterns of habit.

The toughest of all patterns, woven into the gene fabric during our race's distant prehuman existence, is that of the hunting pack, based upon the territorial instinct that has followed man through all his attempts at community. For the primitive pack the combination of inward loyalty and outward aggressiveness was a powerful biological force for survival. As preserved in our nation-states of today it has become one of the major obstacles to even the mere survival of the human species—not to mention its happiness.

No one has ever seen a nation. But just as we see how the trees are bowed by the invisible wind, we see the effects by which each nation manifests itself. Behind the manifestations stand individuals of flesh and blood who tend to feel, think, and act more or less collectively, often in accordance with a pattern specific to the group. The nation-state's raison d'être has been its supposed usefulness for protecting the common interests of the individuals living their lives on a particular piece of territory—the old pack pattern writ large.

The world has now become too small for the hunting-pack mentality. When a creature with deep-rooted aggressive instincts has exchanged his club for a weapon that can sterilize the entire planet, mankind plays a gigantic game of Russian roulette. The risk that the fatal shot will go off may seem small in this particular conflict or that, but as the game continues—if we allow it to continue—it is mathematically certain that the big bang must come some time. With increased crowding and global hunger, and with stiffening rivalry for access to the closed storeroom's limited supplies, conflicts between different super-packs can be raised to hitherto unexperienced dimensions.

Given mankind's present situation, no future social policy—starting now—can make sense that is not based upon men's relations with the total environment. From an ecological standpoint, the nation-states are artificial constructions.

Our treatment of the biosphere, our population growth, our social organization—all are aspects of the same problem. It will probably not be possible to assure a peaceful coexistence within mankind, and to bring about a stewardship of the planet that brings man and his surroundings into balance with each other, without some form of world governance.

Utopia? Maybe. Utopia or possibility—in the end, it comes down to a question of our values and perspectives.

When the first men on the moon looked out into space, they thought the earth—the blue planet—unbelievably beautiful, but also very far away and very small. Perhaps one might expect that the blue speck in limitless space would seem insignificant. The contrary was the case. The astronauts have related that they were struck with its likeness to an island, "the only island that we know is a suitable home for man." They added that they had never felt more strongly the importance of protecting and saving this home.

He sees clearly who sees from afar, dimly who is caught in the details, noted the wise Lao-tzu, in his lonely hut in Han-kuan some hundreds of years before the Christian era. To grasp his local situation, man needs today as never before to see himself from an outside and distant perspective.

There he stands, the primate who came down from the tree! Remarkable his saga, strange what his hunger for knowledge and thirst to learn have brought him to. From the surface of the earth he has lifted himself, toward earth's neighbors in the solar system he steers his spaceship; with artificial eyes he explores distant galaxies, and with artificial ears he listens to reverberations from worlds that lie billions of light-years beyond the cosmic horizon. He can overtake the speed of sound, and he is approaching the speed of light. He can liberate energy that is only to be found in the suns, he can produce elements that nature herself never delivered, and in his test tubes he is beginning to imitate creation's own processes.

All these things are expressions of a technological evolution that increasingly overshadows biological evolution and has made man's development different from that of other earthly creatures. The pace of this development quickened greatly in the middle of the last century, when science and technology joined their functions. Technological evolution has placed its seal on man and all his works, upon his consciousness of self, which we call civilization, upon the integration of minds, which we call society.

But something has been lacking. Even as we have peered out into space with our giant eyes and taken in the voices of the cosmos with our giant ears, we have answered to the picture that Aeschylus had his Prometheus give of primitive mankind: they "had eyes but saw to no purpose; they had ears but did not hear." Despite Copernicus and radio astronomy, in our unreflecting thoughts Terra has remained the pivot of everything. Despite Darwin, we still act as if we stood aside from and above everything else in nature. Ignorance's boon companion has been an arrogance toward the rest of nature, arrogance that has led us inexorably to the present crisis.

Looking backward, the increasing dominance of technological development seems to have been foreshadowed by the brain's and the hand's abilities, which the primate acquired in the treetops and which, when he changed to a ground-level existence, he had to develop further in order to survive. Now that technological development, through its one-sidedness and its acceleration, has driven us near the brink of self-destruction, it is plain that we must emphasize some other route of development.

What will happen next—what must happen if there is to be any "next"? Perhaps it is in a continued evolution of the mind that our eventual future lies. Is there really any other route we can travel to fulfil ourselves?

The planet has only so recently become a place for thinking; mind, evolved out of a unicellular organism's vague trace of irritability, has only so recently ascended to conscious mind, that we may well surmise that we are at the beginning, not the end, of this particular route of development. An extraterrestrial observer of the earthly panorama could reasonably expect that, out of the planet's substance and with man as the medium, there should evolve ever more mind.

Conscious mind—it enters the picture when mind becomes aware of its own existence. It gives a detached perspective that permits the observer to observe himself and thus it becomes a guide to overview and self-knowledge. In these terms, man's conscious mind ought to have a dawn's unexploited possibilities.

As to what new worlds a continued voyage of discovery on such a course might lead mankind—how presumptuous it would be even to speculate! Just as Columbus found another world than the one he looked for, so might an evolving mind lead man to horizons far beyond our present power even to imagine.

What one dares to believe is that heightened mind must surely lead to new discoveries and must itself be shaped by new discoveries in the human spirit and in that cosmos in whose processes the human mind probably plays a role in various ways. The more man-the-seeker discovers about the great cycles of the universe, about the fate of galaxies and the forces in interstellar fields, and perhaps about dimensions and relations that our thought is not yet capable of understanding, the more strongly can man's whole attitude toward life be affected by the exhilaration of taking an observing, probing, and at the same time conscious bit part in the great drama. In mind's continuing evolution an emotional and intellectual adventure might await us that would expose the ideal of the technological era as something utterly primitive and brutal.

In such light, all those ideas of his "uniqueness" that man has cultivated must surely disperse like pale mists over autumnal waters. No part can be meaningful that is separated from the whole.

Just recently a research team at an American university made a penetrating study of man and his needs, only to find that man, like the other mammals, is genetically programed for a state of nature—for clean air, for shifting colors (especially various nuances of green) in the landscape, and for the movements and sounds of other animals around him, not least those of birds. In our heated dwellings, surrounding ourselves with potted plants and a house pet or two, we try unconsciously to recapture something of the tropical savannah of our evolutionary past. For optimum mental health, we must allow our bodies and minds to react in the ways in which a hundred million years of development have equipped them to react.

It might be good to have some evidence of that. You yourself, as you strolled in the fields, have wordlessly felt the secret bonds of union between nature and the processes of your mind. The closer you come to the roots of your existence, the stronger your feeling of unearned peace.

The path inward, the path back. Our paradox is that, in order to achieve inner balance and health, we must rediscover something that harmonizes with our deepest biological needs and, simultaneously, must free ourselves from biological behavior patterns that once helped the species to survive but now tend to have just the opposite effect. It is in fulfilling these seemingly contradictory demands that man can find a way to effect his continued evolution. He must recognize the primeval powers that move through the underbrush of his inner landscape, if ever he is to tame them. But he must also affirm that it is not in a symbiotic relationship with the machines he himself has made, but in being faithful to his deepest biological requirements, that his future may lie. Through enlarged knowledge of ourselves and of the universe surrounding us, we should be able, in a new dimension and under the guidance of conscious mind, to rediscover something of the harmony with nature's creative forces that primitive man felt intuitively and translated into animistic concepts.

Nothing in nature is freely at man's disposal. A tree that began to sprout long before you were born and that will continue to leaf out and unleaf long after your name has been forgotten—how should you be able to "own" it? The living soil, in which microbes and worms break down the remains of life in order to create new possibilities of life; the water, which wanders through its constant circular course from oceans to clouds, from clouds to earth, from earth to flowing water and again out into the oceans; the oxygen-drenched envelope of air around the globe—how should any individual, any generation, any nation, any species be able to own any part of all this?

We are at best only stewards, during a fleeting fragment of time, of something we share with other forms of life, something that has existed since life began and will exist long after we ourselves have expired.

The high ethical imperatives that have been held up to mankind for so long have preached a human brotherhood across all divisions of race, nation, and language. Never have these imperatives been felt more compellingly than now. Just as myriads of independent cell-creatures work together in the individual's body, so must individuals work together as independent components within the body of the global community.

But an ethic that embraces mankind's internal relationships exclusively is only half an ethic. A real one must include everything else in creation. Looking at it this way, we surely have a lot to make amends for!

Viewing our own existence from the vantage point of the stars, the entire earthly biosphere may seem a single organism in which man exists and can exist only in relation to air and water and microbes and plants and animals—all part of an integrated life structure, a structure of dynamic changeability, process, and flow.

Heightened mind must deepen our solidarity with life—as totality, as cosmic phenomenon.

We know something about what we may *not* do

with our world. What we need to learn is how, in cooperation with nature's other forces, we may best function as its steward.

There are signs that new attitudes are on the way.

Within a short time, public opinion has been awakened, especially in the industrial countries, to some comprehension of the environmental threat. More and more often what used to be applauded as "progress" is now received with doubt, sometimes with resistance. A decade ago the concern of a few enthusiasts, environmental preservation has now become practical policy, though the actions currently being taken are still cruelly inadequate. Through the United Nations, a first attempt is being made to get a *global* grip on the issues.

A genuine dissatisfaction with the present system and a desire for new forms of social communion probably underlie the protest movements of youth, which an older generation has no right to wave away just because some of youth's pronouncements seem hard to interpret. Even if some of these are vague and much is yet unclear (as always happens when something is fermenting), there is real promise in youth's will for engagement, in their unconditional internationalism (which leads to various manifestations spreading like wildfire across all ideological boundaries), and in their demonstrative contempt for the GNP-Society's status display.

Even their cultivation of nakedness—a scandal to many of their elders—may be a kind of recapitulation of man's origins. Mircea Eliade, who is prominent in the field of comparative religion, has said that many of the so-called hippies seem to be rediscovering the sacred quality of nature (viz. "the experience of walking around naked among the trees").

In a recent demonstration of environmental activism in Stockholm, young people established themselves on the limbs of a clump of elms and lived in these trees for some days—a desperate attempt to save the trees, which were under a municipal death sentence to make way for a subway entrance. In this, one almost seemed to see a symbolic return to man's primeval treetop home.

All through the affluent industrial countries one sees how people who have never had so much to enjoy have never enjoyed everything less. This may be because they are coming seriously to believe, consciously or unconsciously, that we are on the way to "sacrificing the tree of life to the sales charts of commerce," as someone put it. Even economists, some of them, are making bold to question the holy Gross National Product and to search for other measures of the quality of life. Out of the laboratories and observatories stream ever more studies intended to revolutionize our ways of thinking.

Even if the signs point more than one way, there may be something anticipatory and expectant in all this. At all earlier crossroads in man's history, men have stepped forward who were able to articulate the unexpressed and often hardly perceived wishes, dreams, and needs of their contemporaries. Those who changed people's ways of thinking changed history's course. A wanderer from a generation that has failed at nearly everything worthwhile listens eagerly for voices that can come only from a new generation: preachers who can formulate electrifying appeals, who can, with real passion, exhort us to reflect.

Straining harder than we have ever strained before will be necessary if we are to get through this crisis. Such effort will be impossible unless it proceeds from a positive, sustaining point of view. What we need is an all-embracing philosophy that gathers up mankind's scattered knowledge—from astronomy and anthropology, ecology and ethology, genetics and depth psychology—into a unified and unifying picture of the universe, of life, and of our own fate.

Nature is integration and interaction. The division of natural events into separate compartments is man's invention. It has probably been inevitable that the constantly increased supply of knowledge has led to ever more rigid specializations. But all specialization easily distracts our attention from the simple and the essential. Who stares most sees least; narrow views cramp thought. The more rigid the specialization, the greater the risk of losing the forest in a multitude of trees.

A forest is simple, though its trees be many and each one complex. It is the simplicity of the unifying overview that we must seek. Whatever path you try, you keep coming back to this, because evolution, despite its endless variation, is ultimately unifying.

Everything has evolved out of the mysteriously simple hydrogen atom, with its single proton and its single electron. The multimillion-degree heat of suns has been required to burn hydrogen into helium, the flaming explosions of novae have been required to transform helium into oxygen, the supernovaes' incomprehensible billions of degrees of heat have been required to change oxygen to iron. Out of the simple have all things issued, even the most complex; and out of the minutest constituents have the solar systems and galaxies evolved.

Into that cosmic evolution, biological evolution on certain heavenly bodies fits as a fragment. Within that fragment, hydrogen has primordially evolved into, among other things, the species to which we belong.

The road was long, but the route was clear. What staggers us is that the cosmic substance within us can *know* that it is united with all that went before, not only on this earth but also in the processes of space from which the elements came that built up the earth and its life—and that the same substance, as conscious mind, can itself strive toward the stars. Learning to understand this involves more than merely recording experiences and observations, important as these are as the backbone of a viable philosophy. Were the word not so easily associated with tribal gods and with confessions, one might dare to speak of a "religious" attitude that embraces protons and electrons as well as galaxies, amino acids as well as the subtlest visions of our brains.

Perhaps it is through learning to understand such a unifying simplicity that we can evolve into what we have presumptuously believed ourselves to be: Homo *sapiens.*

The wanderer among earth's trees grasps at maybes, at the most far-fetched eventualities. As one of the human species, he feels it absurdly unreal that this race, descendant of hydrogen atoms, supernovae, and uncountable aeons, should now be on the verge of wiping itself out while the possibility still remains that man's free will can choose continued development.

To illusions let there be no more sacrifices! So great are the demands being placed on mankind's collective flexibility and self-control that failure seems all too easy. Man's numbers are against him already, and time is also not on his side.

Nor can man kindle with the hope of finding, beyond the crisis haply surmounted, a world where some "dreams i' th' bud grow flowers." Such worlds have never existed and will never exist except as destinations for our flights from reality.

But it was another force that drove man forward in spite of everything. Through all his wandering, the call of the unknown led him into constantly new domains. Once, it lured him across the earth, up to the highest peaks and down to the greatest ocean depths, and it has persuaded him to brave the heat of the deserts and the cold of the poles; now, it lures him away from the planet.

Those unknown possibilities the future can offer our evolving mind—should they not exert a power capable of persuading humankind to submit to just such labors as its pioneers have accomplished in humanity's moments of greatness?

The wanderer grasps at a last maybe.

Above the earth we raised ourselves, once, and became men. It happened mostly in the face of probability. Could we be inspired with a sense that evolution has just confronted our species with a planetary test, unique in this part of the universe but repeated at innumerable other points throughout infinite immensity, might that raise us to previously unexampled heights of humility and tenacity, responsibility and passion?

Providing thereby new starting points for continued wandering?

BIBLIOGRAPHICAL NOTE

Material for the thoughts in this book has been taken from many different places: newspapers and specialized journals, conversations and books. To assist the reader who may wish to go further, a list is given here of some of the books that have directly or indirectly furnished background material to the author, and of some additional titles, most of them published since the Swedish edition appeared, considered by the editor to be of related interest. The list is limited to works that are accessible to the general reader in English. Titles added by the editor are marked with an asterisk.

Alland, Alexander, Jr.: *The Human Imperative (New York, 1972); Alfvén, Hannes: Worlds-Antiworlds (San Francisco, 1966); Allen, J. David, and A. J. Hanson, eds.: *Recycle This Book! Ecology, Society, and Man (Belmont, Cal., 1972); Ardrey, Robert: The Territorial Imperative (New York, 1966); Arendt, Hannah: The Human Condition (Chicago, 1970); Aron, Raymond: Industrial Society (New York, 1967); Arthur, Don R.: Man and His Environment (New York, 1969).

Bates, M.: Man in Nature (New York, 1964); Bateson, Mary Catherine: *Our Own Metaphor (New York, 1972); Baumer, Franklin L.: Religion and the Rise of Skepticism (New York, 1960); Bird, Caroline: *The Crowding Syndrome (New York, 1972); Borgström, Georg: *Too Many, A Study of Earth's Biological Limitations (New York, 1969); Brower, David R., ed.: *Only a Little Planet (New York, 1972); Brown, Lester: Seeds of Change (New York, 1970).

Calder, Nigel: Eden Was No Garden (New York, 1967), Technopolis (New York, 1970); Carroll, John B.: Language and Thought (Englewood Cliffs, N. J., 1964); Carthy, J. D.: The Study of Behavior (New York, 1966); Cassirer, Ernst: An Essay on Man (New York, 1964); Chase, Allan: *The Biological Imperatives (Baltimore, 1973); Chomsky, Noam: Language and Mind (New York, 1968); Commoner, Barry: Science and Survival (New York, 1966); Costello, D. F.: *The Desert World (New York, 1972); Critchlow, Keith: *Into the Hidden Environment: The Oceans (New York, 1973).

Darnell, Rezneat M.: *Organism and Environment: A Manual of Quantitative Ecology (San Francisco, 1971); De Bell, Garrett: The Environmental Handbook (New York, 1970); Dubos, René: *A God Within (New York, 1972).

Edberg, Rolf: On the Shred of a Cloud: Notes in a Travel Book (University, Al., 1969); Ehrlich, Paul: *The Population Bomb (New York, 1968) and, with Anne H. Ehrlich, *Population, Resources, *and Environment: Issues in Human Ecology* (San Francisco, 1970); Eiseley, Loren: **The Night Country* (New York, 1972); Environment Information Center: **The Environment Index* (New York, 1972); Environmental Studies Board of the National Academy of Sciences: **Institutional Arrangements for International Environmental Cooperation* (Washington, D. C., 1972).

Ferkiss, Victor C.: *Technological Man* (New York, 1969); French, Herbert E.: **Love of Earth* (New York, 1972); Fuller, R. Buckminster, et al.: **Approaching the Benign Environment* (University, Al., 1970).

Garrett, Hardin: **Exploring the New Ethics for Survival: The Voyage of the Space Ship Beagle* (New York, 1972); Gorney, Roderic: **The Human Agenda* (New York, 1972); Graham, Frank, Jr.: **Where the Place Called Morning Lies* (New York, 1973).

Hardin, G., ed.: **Population, Evolution, and Birth Control* (San Francisco, 1969); Hawkins, Gerald S.: *Beyond Stonehenge* (New York, 1973); Hayakawa, S. I.: *Our Language and Our World* (New York, 1959); Heisenberg, Werner: **Across the Frontiers* (New York, 1973); Helfrich, Harold., Jr.: *Agenda for Survival* (New Haven, 1970), **The Environmental Crisis: Man's Struggle to Live with Himself* (New Haven, 1970); Herzberg, Frederick: *Work and the Nature of Man* (New York, 1966); Hinton, John: *Dying* (Baltimore, 1968); Huth, Hans: **Nature and the Americans: Three Centuries of Changing Attitudes* (Lincoln, Neb., 1972); Huxley, Julian: *Religion Without Revelation* (New York, 1958).

Jaspers, Karl: *The Origin and Goal of History* (New Haven, 1953).

Kahn, Herman, and B. Bruce-Briggs: **Things to Come* (New York, 1972); Kaufman, Walter: **Without Guilt and Justice* (New York, 1973); Kay, Dard A., and Eugene B. Skolnikoff, eds.: **World Eco-Crisis: International Organizational in Response* (Madison, Wisc., 1972); Kopal, Zdenek: **Man and His Universe* (New York, 1972); Krutch, Joseph Wood: **The Great Chain of Life* (Boston, 1957); Kurtén, Björn: **Not from the Apes* (New York, 1972).

Lapp, Ralph E.: **The Logarithmic Century* (New York, 1973); Leach, Edmund: *A Runaway World?* (New York, 1968); Le Gros Clark, Sir Wilfrid E.: *Man-apes or Ape-men* (New York, 1967); Leiss, William: **The Domination of Nature* (New York, 1972); Lewis, John, and Bernhard Towers: *Naked Ape or Homo sapiens* (New York, 1969); Lorenz, Konrad: *Studies in Animal and Human Behavior*

(London, 1970), *On Aggression* (New York, 1965); Luria, S. E.: *Life—The Unfinished Experiment* (New York, 1973); Lutz, P. E., and H. Santmire: **Ecological Renewal* (New York, 1972).

McHale, John: *The Future of the Future* (New York, 1969); Madariaga, Salvador de: *Portrait of a Man Standing* (University, Al., 1968); Maddox, John: **The Doomsday Syndrome* (New York, 1972); Marine, Gene: **America the Raped* (New York, 1969); Marquand, Josephine: *Life: Its Nature, Origins, and Distribution* (New York, 1968); Matthiesson, Peter, and Eliott Porter: **The Tree Where Man Was Born/The African Experience* (New York, 1972); Meadows, Donella, Dennis L. Meadows, Jorgen Randers, and William W. Behrens II: **The Limits to Growth* (Washington, D. C., 1972); Mishan, T. J.: *Technology and Growth* (New York, 1970); Milne, Lorus, and Margery Milne: **The Animal in Man* (New York, 1973); Mitchell, John G., and Constance L. Stallings, eds.: **Ecotactics: The Sierra Club Handbook for Environmental Activists* (New York, 1970); Monod, Jacques: **Chance and Necessity: An Essay on the Natural Philosophy of Modern Biology* (New York, 1971); Morgan, Elaine: **The Descent of Woman* (New York, 1972); Morris, Desmond: *The Naked Ape* (New York, 1967), *The Human Zoo* (New York, 1969); Mott, Francis J.: *The Universal Design of Creation* (Bedford, 1964); Myrdal, Gunnar: *Challenge of World Poverty* (New York, 1970).

Novic, Sheldon: *Carless Atom* (Boston, 1969).

Odum, Eugene: *Ecology* (New York, 1966); Ortega y Gasset, José: **Meditations on Hunting* (New York, 1972); Overman, Michael: *Water* (Garden City, 1969); Ovington, J. D.: *Woodlands* (London, 1966).

Platt, John R.: *The Step to Man* (New York, 1966).

Roslansky, J. D., ed.: **The Control of the Environment* (New York, 1972); Rostand, Jean: **A Biologist's Notes on the Future of Mankind* (New York, 1973); Rudd, Robert L.: *Pesticides and the Living Landscape* (Madison, Wis., 1964); Russell, Claire, and W. S. Russell: *Violence, Monkeys, and Man* (London, 1968).

Sakahrov, Andrei: *Progress, Coexistence, and Intellectual Freedom* (New York, 1968); Schaller, George B.: **The Serengeti Lion: A Study of Predator-Prey Relations* (Chicago, 1972); Shapley, Harlow: *View from a Distant Star* (New York, 1965); Sherrington, Sir Charles: *Man on His Nature* (Cambridge, 1963); Shweidman, Edwin S: **Deaths of Man* (New York, 1973); Simpson, George Gaylord: *Tempo and Mode in Evolution* (New York, 1965); Strahler, A. N.: **Planet Earth: Its Physical Systems through Geologic Time* (New York, 1972).

Taylor, Gordon R.: *The Biological Time Bomb* (New York, 1968) and *The Doomsday Book* (New York, 1970); Theobald, Robert: **Habit and Habitat* (New York, 1972); Toffler, Alvin: *Future Shock* (New York, 1970); Toynbee, Arnold, et al.: *Man's Concern with Death* (New York, 1969); Turnbull, Colin M.: **The Mountain People* (New York, 1972).

Vacca, Robert: **The Coming Dark Age* (New York, 1973).

Ward, Barbara, and René Dubos: **Only One Earth: The Care and Maintenance of a Small Planet* (New York, 1972); Watson, James D.: *The Double Helix* (New York, 1968); Weisman, Avery D.: **On Dying and Denying* (New York, 1972); Winton, H.N.M., comp. and ed.: **Man and the Environment: A Bibliography of Selected Publications of the United Nations System, 1946-1971* (New York, 1972).